WITHDRAWN
UTSA LIBRARIES

D0223085

On
Shame

Participating in a recent revival of philosophical interest in the phenomenon of shame and its relation to our identities and practical lives, Michael Morgan's book makes a passionate and philosophically intelligent case for regarding shame as fundamental to the kinds of social beings we are.

Alice Crary, The New School for Social Research

Deeply engaging and very easy to read. The subject Morgan addresses is timely and important. *On Shame* provides philosophical analysis in a way that should be accessible to the educated reader, and mixes this analysis effectively with current events, literature, film and psychology. It is thoughtful and thought provoking, and speaks to issues of real and immediate concern. I suspect many people will be grateful for the help it provides in thinking more deeply about difficult issues that cannot be ignored.

Marya Schechtman, University of Illinois at Chicago

Praise for the series

'. . . allows a space for distinguished thinkers to write about their passions.'

The Philosophers' Magazine

'. . . deserve high praise.'

Boyd Tonkin, The Independent (UK)

'This is clearly an important series. I look forward to reading future volumes.'

Frank Kermode, author of Shakespeare's Language

'. . . both rigorous and accessible.'

Humanist News

'. . . the series looks superb.'

Quentin Skinner

'. . . an excellent and beautiful series.'

Ben Rogers, author of A.J. Ayer: A Life

'Routledge's *Thinking in Action* series is the theory junkie's answer to the eminently pocketable Penguin 60s series.'

Mute Magazine (UK)

'Routledge's new series, *Thinking in Action*, brings philosophers to our aid . . .'

The Evening Standard (UK)

'. . . a welcome new series by Routledge.'

Bulletin of Science, Technology and Society (Can)

'Routledge's innovative new *Thinking in Action* series takes the concept of philosophy a step further'

The Bookwatch

MICHAEL L. MORGAN

On
Shame

Routledge
Taylor & Francis Group

NEW YORK AND LONDON

First published 2008
by Routledge
270 Madison Ave, New York, NY 10016

Simultaneously published in the UK
by Routledge
2 Park Square, Milton Park, Abingdon, Oxon OX14 4RN

Routledge is an imprint of the Taylor & Francis Group, an informa business

© 2008 Taylor & Francis

Typeset in Joanna MT and Din by
RefineCatch Ltd, Bungay, Suffolk
Printed and bound in the United States of America on acid-free paper by
Edwards Brothers

All rights reserved. No part of this book may be reprinted or
reproduced or utilized in any form or by any electronic,
mechanical, or other means, now known or hereafter
invented, including photocopying and recording, or in any
information storage or retrieval system, without permission in
writing from the publishers.

Trademark Notice: Product or corporate names may be trademarks or registered
trademarks, and are used only for identification and explanation without intent to
infringe.

Library of Congress Cataloging in Publication Data
A catalog record has been requested for this book

ISBN10: 0–415–39622–0 (hbk)
ISBN10: 0–415–39623–9 (pbk)
ISBN10: 0–203–93243–9 (ebk)

ISBN13: 978–0–415–39622–6 (hbk)
ISBN13: 978–0–415–39623–3 (pbk)
ISBN13: 978–0–203–93243–8 (ebk)

**Library
University of Texas
at San Antonio**

Preface

This book is about the emotion of shame. It proposes and then discusses how shame can be called upon as a motivation for moral development, especially as a response to the horrific genocides of the past century. Shame is one of a family of self-conscious emotions that includes embarrassment, guilt, disgrace, and humiliation. Some psychologists have even suggested that the word "shame" be used for this entire family of emotions as well as for one member of it. In the first chapter, I introduce the discussion by sketching a "narrative," as it were, of how I came to feel shame about living in a world of genocide and atrocity and how that feeling is complicated by the litany of horrors that mark the past century and also by various modes of representation that have influenced my sense of our place in such a world. In the subsequent chapters I draw out three strands from that initial sketch. In the second chapter I discuss shame in general, its relationships with other similar emotions, and the special kind of shame I have in mind. In the third chapter, I reflect upon how shame about atrocity and genocide is complicated and ramified by our reactions to the ways we learn about them, especially to literary and cinematic representations of these events. Finally, in the fourth chapter, I discuss how people respond to shame and specifically how shame can become a motivation for moral development.

The book began with an essay I wrote at the invitation of John K. Roth for *Genocide and Human Rights*. Simon Critchley suggested I expand it into a book on shame. I was also encouraged by Deborah Wilkes, Joshua Shaw, and Mira Wasserman, all of whom read the original essay and found something valuable in it. Tony Bruce and Kate Ahl at Routledge gave me good advice about the direction the book might take and about clarifying the book's argument. In addition, three readers for Routledge provided me with helpful comments and questions on an earlier draft, many of which I have attempted to deal with. As I have been working on the book, numerous friends have suggested literary and cinematic examples of moments of shame that might be useful; I am indebted to them but of course my use of those examples is solely my responsibility.

Finally, I would like to thank my family—Sara and Marc, Debbie and Adam—for the interest they always take in my work and the joy they have brought Aud and myself, a joy now immeasurably increased with the birth of Gabrielle and Sasha. Looking into their eyes, I am filled with wonder and a hope beyond hope that their world will be a better place to be.

Introduction

The emotional state of shame is a complex and fascinating emotion and one that has special significance for us today. Present in our lives in a variety of ways and in a variety of circumstances, it has attracted widespread attention. Psychologists have studied its multifaceted and fascinating career. Philosophers have analyzed its structure and character. Novelists, poets, and other artists have exposed its nuances and power. Journalists have bemoaned its effects on the persecuted, the oppressed, and the desperate. Indeed, some have attributed much of the violence and anger that characterize our world to the ubiquity of shame and its dominance over us.

Through such vast and complex territory, this short book traces a very precise path. It makes a claim about one role that shame might play for us and provides a preliminary articulation of that claim. The claim is a moral one, that shame is an emotional state that we should elicit for ourselves as one aspect of our response to the situation in which we find ourselves. That situation is marked by the occurrence of an array of human atrocities during the past several decades, atrocities that are genocidal in character and scope, atrocities characterized by brutality, violence, and systematic annihilation. The claim I make in the book is that in response to such atrocities we ought collectively to cultivate in ourselves a sense of shame for allowing such acts to occur and to continue to occur, that this sense of shame is distinctive for several reasons, that it is complicated by the ways in which these atrocities are represented to us and communicated to us through art and cinema—among other ways, and that this shame can and should lead to lives committed to preventing such atrocities from continuing to occur. If ours is a genocidal world, then we should do something about changing it; we should care that acts of mass slaughter and massacre take place and do what we can to prevent them.

This book, then, is not a survey of what we understand about shame, nor is it a philosophical analysis of its features and structure. Rather I claim that we should feel shame about a prominent feature of our world and use that shame to motivate us to act. It is in this sense that the character of the book is ethical; it is about an ethical response to the world we live in.

There is much that is controversial about the point I try to make. Shame is an emotional state that overcomes us when certain kinds of circumstances occur. We do not normally think of it as voluntary, as a state that we enact, as it were. Yet I claim that we can come to feel shame by choosing to do so. Furthermore, shame is typically focused on a feature that we have or are thought to have, or an action that we have performed or are said to have performed. But here the shame I discuss is focused not on a personal feature or an action but rather on neglect or indifference. Moreover, it is a neglect or indifference that is not ours privately, so to speak, but something that we share collectively, as members of a society or people or indeed as members of humankind. We normally think of shame as a private emotion, one that we have on our own, but in this book I speak of a shame that we share with others, with members of our group, of our nation, and of all humankind. It is unusual to speak of shame in this way, but I think that we can and should. These are three of several features of this special shame that are not typical, but they are plausible. And there are more such features, which I discuss in the course of the book.

Our world is plagued by many problems worthy of our concern—the plight of the impoverished and the hungry, misuse of the environment and failure to appreciate the consequences of global warming, the oppression and persecution of women and minorities, and a host of others. It is surely the case that neglect or indifference with respect to any number of these problems is worth our attention, and it may be that cultivating the kind of shame I have in mind would be important in order to motivate serious and responsible action aimed at solving these problems.[1] In this book, however, I have selected one problem among these many, the problem of genocidal brutality and the degradations that accompany such brutality. I claim that for us now, not perpetrators but bystanders, in order to move us to action, we ought to feel ashamed at living in a world that has conducted such actions and continues to allow them to occur. Guilt will not do, nor fear or anger, but shame will, as I explain.

Like guilt, shame is a powerful emotion. Why is it especially worth our cultivating shame for humankind for the frequency and violence of genocides? I do not think that we can or should engage in comparing the relative dangers and ills of genocides, the misuse of nature, persecution and oppression of minorities, gender prejudice, and such. Many of these problems are certainly serious worldwide problems. They and others like them have contributed to injustice; they threaten the future well-being of all of us, and they have contributed to lives of poverty, hunger, and despair. Among such ills, however, genocide is especially horrific.

First, genocide is not a product of indifference or neglect, although indifference can surely contribute to it. Rather genocide involves an uncompromising hatred that targets not one person or a random number of persons but an entire people or ethnic group or religious group. Moreover, the goal of genocide is not simply to oppress that group or to malign it; it is to annihilate it completely, both its members and its culture, to eradicate the group and indeed the very memory of it. Furthermore, genocide involves violence of an extreme but calculated kind. It can be executed in crude and brutal ways, with guns or machetes, or it can employ the most advanced technology, but in either case genocide is directed to carry out its designs and is implemented through the mechanisms of government and of organized authority. But if the essence of evil is its negativity, then genocide, because it seeks to eradicate totally, to wipe others from the face of the earth, is the extreme of evil and the anti-human. Thus, if it is characteristic of our contemporary world, then the limit it marks is an extreme one indeed, certainly worth our deepest concern. If our world has come to cultivate types of conduct and ways of being that are worthy of our greatest concern, surely genocide is paramount among them.

Furthermore, historically speaking, the society of nations collectively, after World War II and the Nazi Holocaust, made genocide a matter of explicit international concern and made itself a promise, that even the sanctity of national sovereignty would be no barrier to intervention in order to prevent such events from taking place.[2] And yet, that promise and agreement notwithstanding, the second half of the twentieth century and the beginning of the twenty-first century have seen several genocidal programs carried out. Again and again, we have been reminded of the broken promise and the shame we all should feel—about the failure of allowing these events to occur and about failing to keep the promise that the members of the United Nations once made. My claim that we should feel shame in the face of such failure, then, is no novelty; I am underscoring what many others have said and with good reason.

Most of us are not directly the perpetrators of genocidal atrocities. But we do live in a genocidal world, one that tolerates such acts and one that has regularly failed to intervene to prevent them or to stop them. I claim that to focus our attention and that of our government and the governments of other nations on the need to respond, we ought to feel shame at living in such a world. Shame, as I point out, involves self-criticism. It does not aim at an action per se but rather at the self who feels it, and it recommends, it encourages self-transformation. Ultimately, if our governments and the society of nations are to act to intervene and to prevent such acts, we must see the urgency of so doing, and to see that urgency we must look at others and ourselves in a different way. Shame, as the kind of emotion it is, is appropriate to motivate such changes in ourselves. My choice of shame as the emotional centerpiece of this book is partially grounded in my own personal experience and that of many others, but it is justified too by the very nature of shame, as I try to point out.

I have not organized the book as an argument or defense of this claim about shame and its value. I have instead taken some time, in chapter 1, to set forth the claim, and then in chapters 2 through 4, to articulate or elaborate it. This is not to say that I say nothing to defend it. I do. But what defense or argument there is takes place within the course of this articulation or elaboration. Hence the book has this structure. In chapter 1, I introduce the claim in a somewhat auto-biographical way. In chapter 2, I clarify what shame is, what distinguishes this kind of shame, and how shame differs from other emotional states often associated with it—guilt, embarrassment, humiliation, and disgrace. In chapter 3, I introduce a complexity in our eliciting shame in ourselves for failing to take genocidal brutality seriously and responsibly. Given where we stand, the horrors of these events are conveyed to us in many ways—literary, cinematic, journalistic, and more. In this chapter, I discuss how modes of representation can in fact add dimensions of shame to the shame of neglect and indifference. To be sure, when a book or film distorts or camouflages the horrific, we can react emotionally in many ways, but I claim that when the issue is the horrors of genocide, and if the emotion we elicit in that regard is shame, then the emotional response to such distortions and misrepresentations is also shame.

Finally, in chapter 4, I note that while shame is often a reaction and is here a response, it is not intended to be the whole of our response. Rather my proposal is that we elicit shame in order to motivate ourselves to respond directly to oppose the atrocities and to do what we can—individually, collectively, politically, morally—to prevent genocides from occurring and to intervene when they do and to respond to the needs of their victims with commitment and vigor. Given the generality of the book's theme, there is not much detail in this chapter; such details depend upon the particular circumstances, needs, and possibilities, that attend such events—for example, those that existed at the time of the Rwandan genocide and those that now characterize the genocide in Darfur. My point here is to locate shame within a larger conception of response to genocide and to emphasize that the emotional response is primarily a motivation to act.

In order to trace this path through the emotional territory associated with shame, I call attention to the ways that shame has been discussed by psychologists, philosophers, and in the arts. The book presents one perspective for viewing this terrain. At the same time, my primary intent has not been descriptive or expository. In the sense that I have explained, my goal is a moral and practical one.

One

Ten years after the Third Reich was defeated and the Nazi death camps were liberated, Alain Resnais was persuaded to create a film about their horrors and atrocities. *Night and Fog* was the result of his subsequent collaboration with Jean Cayrol, who wrote the narration, and Hanns Eisler, who composed the film's musical score.[1] The central theme of this remarkable film is that, appearances notwithstanding, the evil of the death camps and of Nazi fascism remained alive in France in 1955. It might have seemed to the film's original audiences that the evil and the horror had been destroyed with the liberation of the camps and with the end of the ruthless empire of death, but Resnais' and Cayrol's message was that they had not. Time might have deposited layers of debris over the past; life might have continued, hiding not only that past but also the agencies of evil that existed in the present, in 1955. The lesson of *Night and Fog*, however, is that while time may make forgetfulness easy and memory difficult, this means that memory becomes a challenge and a task.[2] Forgetfulness goes hand in hand with a terrifying threat, that today and tomorrow, again and again, we will be made to live once more as agents, victims, or bystanders of such atrocities. If those alive in 1955 did not remember the past, then the forces of degradation and inhumanity would continue to win their victories, and we will all be their victims.

I was led to think about *Night and Fog* in 2004 when I watched *Ghosts of Rwanda*, a television documentary broadcast by PBS on the tenth anniversary of the Rwandan genocide, which largely took place in one hundred days from April to July in 1994. I do not mean to compare the latter film, an historical and educational documentary, to *Night and Fog*, which many regard as the greatest non-fiction film ever made. Cinematically there is no comparison. Nonetheless, seeing the new film brought the older one to mind. As I watched *Ghosts of Rwanda* and listened to the people interviewed, many of whom I had read about—victims, politicians, doctors, United Nations officials, and others—I recalled how often, in the books on the Rwandan genocide, the Nazi Holocaust was invoked as a standard and a warning, as the origin for the agreements and promises that Rwanda—and not it alone—showed us and the world to be breaking. In reflecting on the juxtaposition of the two events, I thought about the juxtaposition of living ten years after the one event and then after the other. I considered what I feel now, what Resnais may have felt then, what he hoped his audience would feel, then and thereafter, and where history leaves me and us, where we have come and where we have failed, and how and where we stand today.

When I speak of *we* and *us*, how should those terms be understood? First and most generally, *we* may refer to humankind. Second and more specifically, I have in mind people in Western nations whose lives have coincided with the Holocaust and subsequent genocides, those of us who have lived through these catastrophes or have learned about them through reading, film, and other media, those of us who are bewildered and deeply upset at where we and Western civilization stand. Third, since I am a philosopher, *we* and *us* also refer to the community of philosophers and thus to philosophy itself. In this respect, I ask where philosophy stands today in a world in which the Holocaust and subsequent genocides have taken place and in which genocidal acts continue to occur. What I say here applies to all three of these understandings of we and us.

THE COST OF FORGETFULNESS

Night and Fog is not an account of the rise of Nazis and the creation of the death camps. Resnais and Cayrol use images, narration, and music to raise questions, to expose evidence to the viewer and to provoke reflection, to elicit our responses and then to unsettle them, to get us to think about how we see and understand what took place. A central theme of this process is the ease of missing what is placed before us, of failing to recognize what we see, of being blinded or having our senses dulled, so that the past is taken as settled, dead, gone, and irrelevant. In the film, the use of color along with black and white, the simplicity of Cayrol's comments and questions and the almost monotonous quality of the narrator's voice, and the gentle lyricism of much of Eisler's music—all tempt us to let the evidence flow by, to glide over the threatening nature of Nazi fascism and the atrocities it produced as they are depicted in the film's photographs and archival footage. But at the same time, the dissonance of what we see and how it is presented is intended to unsettle us about our responses and about those temptations. We should leave our viewing disturbed and warned.

In the literature about the Rwandan genocide, references to the Nazis and to the Holocaust regularly call attention to the warning "Never again" as the paradigmatic response to the death camps and Nazi terror.[3] In 1955, in France, Resnais and

Cayrol realized that it would be easy not to appreciate the importance of such a warning, of committing ourselves to it and remembering it. In a sense, the primary intention of *Night and Fog* is to restore the past and register the importance of the warning against forgetfulness. It is not that we, who live after Auschwitz, would not *want* to avoid a repetition of such horrors. Surely, once we realized what had happened at Auschwitz, we would want to prevent anything like it from occurring again. The issue was that one might not see that such a commitment was necessary because it would seem to be irrelevant. One might deny that the conditions for such atrocities are still present or fail to read the signs correctly or ignore the signs when they are there. Or, even more sadly and more terribly, one might have the signs pointed out or even the occurrence identified and still refuse to accept that what was happening was a repetition of what happened under Nazism. There are many ways, Resnais seems to be saying, in which we might be tempted to avoid our commitments—to humanity and to particular human beings and to the victims of the death camps.

Ghosts of Rwanda is a different sort of film. It is not artful but informational and educational, conventional in its use of interviews and reportage. Nevertheless, its point is similar to *Night and Fog*'s. The film about Rwanda reminds the viewer that what took place in 1994 was a genocide, that after the Holocaust the UN in 1948 passed a convention committing the nations of the world to intervene to prevent genocides from occurring, and that Rwanda marks a failure of that commitment. The film reminds the viewer that the genocide in Rwanda may have occurred during a civil war, but that it was a genocide nonetheless, that it included acts of extraordinary brutality and cruelty, and that it was methodically planned and implemented rigorously and efficiently through a mobilization of common people and neighbors under the direction of politicians, government officials, the military, and the media.[4] Moreover, the film reports a failure or a host of failures by individuals, powerful Western nations, and the United Nations. In this regard, *Ghosts of Rwanda* follows the direction of much of the literature on the genocide. Criticisms have been regularly made of a number of individuals, in addition to those who organized and directed the genocide from within the Rwandan political and military institutions, but the most important targets are the leaders of nations—in particular those of Belgium, France, Great Britain, and the United States—and the leadership of the United Nations.

In the cases of the United Nations and the United States, whose role on the Security Council and in the UN is so central, the explanations of why they acted as they did, opposing and avoiding military intervention and obstructing effective assistance for vital periods of time, normally focus on the catastrophe in Somalia and the battle of Mogadishu in the fall of 1993, as well as on the problems that were ongoing in Bosnia and Serbia.[5] But whatever the best explanation of their actions, especially the actions of the United States executive (the State Department, the White House, and the military) and the actions of the UN Secretariat, the fact is that when it was known that a genocide was occurring— organized and executed by the government and under government supervision, with lists of victims having been prepared based on racial considerations, with trained militia to support the military and eventually to take over from them, with the use of radio broadcasting of hate propaganda, and more—everything was done to avoid intervention and even to prevent others from intervening.[6]

The message of *Ghosts of Rwanda*, like that of so much of the literature on the Rwandan genocide, is that when some 800,000 Tutsis were slaughtered in a matter of weeks—the killing's rate surpassed the Nazis' attack on the Jews in that regard—the leadership of the United Nations and the United States stood by, watched, permitted the brutality to go on, refused to intervene, and even prevented others from doing so. Because of their historical relationships with Rwanda, the governments of France and Belgium responded, in some ways, even more culpably. The television film wants its viewers to appreciate that we today are haunted by the "ghosts" of Rwanda—together with those of Cambodia, Bosnia, Kosovo, and, at the time of this writing, by the genocide that is under way in Darfur—and by the warning about what may lie ahead for us if we do not honor the promises we have made to one another.

If *Night and Fog* is about forgetting, then *Ghosts of Rwanda* is about a forgetting mediated by denial. The denial was that of the United Nations, of the United States government, and of many more; it was a denial that the events occurring in Rwanda after April 6, 1994 were genocide. There were those who denied that genocide was going on, some for weeks, others for months. Why? To avoid the obligations and the responsibilities that would accompany this admission, responsibilities and moral demands tied to the United Nations Convention on Genocide. Watching *Ghosts of Rwanda*, then, provokes—or should provoke—shame before what one hears and sees, the images, the interviews, and the admissions, often given, that more should have been done, that the denials were evasions.[7] One ought to feel shame before these confessions, which are often themselves expressions of guilt and shame, but the viewer's shame would echo against the commitments after the Holocaust that led to the United Nations Genocide Convention and then, later, to the UN's problematic role in intervention against genocide. Our shame would be a shame for these denials too; we are ashamed—or should be ashamed, if we are not—of being ones who forget, of being bystanders who did not act in behalf of those in need, and of being deniers or beneficiaries of deniers, even as we today, so many of us, criticize and judge deniers of the Holocaust.

THE SIGNIFICANCE OF SHAME

One cannot, I think, watch the *Ghosts of Rwanda* without a profound sense of sympathy for all those who suffered and who then continued to suffer and for those who suffer to this day, for the victims and survivors of the genocide. We also are horrified by what we see, the brutality of the slaughter; we are angry and we are afraid.[8] But beyond the sympathy, horror, anger, and fear, there is something else. We should, I am proposing, also feel the shame that I have just mentioned.[9] Sympathy is directed toward the victims; shame is directed toward ourselves. If sympathy wants to relieve the suffering and pain of others, it needs this shame that reflects something about how we feel about ourselves and who we are.[10] But what is the character of this shame? And does it tell us anything about how we should live or about what we ought to do in living, now, more than ten years after Rwanda and sixty years after Auschwitz?

Shame is a complex state, emotional and evaluative and hence psychological and ethical at once. It is reflexive and yet social, requiring that we look at ourselves and at the way others view us, at once and dialectically.[11] And while shame is akin to guilt, the two are not identical.[12] We can be ashamed about what we have done, just as we can feel guilty for what we have done, but in such cases shame is about who we are for having done what we did; we are ashamed for having been the one who did what we did.[13] Guilt is related but different. We feel guilty for having done what we did but not for being who we are.

Shame, moreover, involves losing face and caring that we have done so. We lose face before others. It matters to us how others see us, and so we care about how we present ourselves to them. When we are ashamed in this way, we are focused not on what we have done but rather on how our actions or omissions show us to be to others, and we are focused on how they will see us in virtue of that "face" and the way that our action presents us to them. Furthermore, shame may not be about how others actually see us; rather it is about how we think they do or would, as a result of seeing us or looking at us as the ones who acted as we did. What shames us is our own estimate of ourselves, made not from our own perspective, but as our projection based on how others might look at us, given what we know about ourselves as the way they might see us.[14]

In short, shame is our own way of seeing ourselves, not through the prism of our actions, but through the prism of how others would see us in terms of our features or actions. Hence, shame involves a judgment of value about what we think others should think about who we are, given how we have conducted ourselves. But this means that shame requires of us that we have some notion of how we should be or ought to be, the kind of person we ought to be, and the kind of person others ought to expect us to be, in terms of which our actions show us to have failed, to be deficient, to be diminished. When we are ashamed, we have lost face because the face we value and hope to have has been displaced or defaced by another face, which is one that we regret having, one that disgraces or embarrasses us.[15]

All of this depth and complexity is to say that shame reaches far into who we take ourselves to be, who we hope to be, and into how we feel about how we are viewed.[16] Hence, shame is a very revealing emotional state, even if it is one that we do not seek to feel. In an important chapter of his book *The Drowned and the Saved*, Primo Levi reflects on the shame of one who survived Auschwitz.[17] Levi's account is not analytical or systematic. What he seeks to disclose are different modes of shame that occurred for him and for other survivors of Auschwitz and what they mean. In order to understand what it would mean for us to feel shame today, we may begin by turning to his thoughts, written in the shadow of Auschwitz.

PRIMO LEVI'S SENSE OF SHAME AND ITS IMPLICATIONS FOR US

Levi's chapter on shame was first published in 1986. Its beginning includes a recollection from his novel *The Reawakening*, which was published in 1963 but written, he says, early in 1947, not long after his return to Turin, Italy. The chapter might be read as a gloss on the passage from the novel, which describes, he says, "the first Russian soldiers facing our Lager packed with corpses and dying prisoners":

> They did not greet us, nor smile; they seemed oppressed, not only by pity but also by a confused restraint which sealed their mouths, and kept their eyes fastened on the funereal scene. It was the same shame which we knew so well, which submerged us after the selections, and every time we had to

witness or undergo an outrage: the shame that the Germans
never knew, the shame which the just man experiences when
confronted by a crime committed by another, and he feels
remorse because of its existence, because of its having been
irrevocably introduced into the world of existing things, and
because his will has proven nonexistent or feeble and was
incapable of putting up a good defense.[18]

Levi's chapter on shame goes on to say that it may sound
strange to learn that he and other inmates of the camps felt
shame and that he wants to interpret it. As victims themselves,
what did they have to be ashamed about?

But the passage just quoted harbors a dialectical turn. His
reflection about shame begins with the observation about his
Russian liberators and their expressions, their actions or
omissions, and their feelings. He sees in them an emotion that
he and other inmates have also felt, which he calls "shame"
and goes on to characterize. Although Levi, for his own
reasons, intended to clarify the dimensions or modes of that
shame as he and other prisoners felt it, I want to ask a different but related question: what can his account, itself a
response to the fact of Auschwitz, tell us about our own
shame, the shame we might feel as we recall Rwanda—and
Cambodia, Bosnia, Kosovo, and Darfur—against the background of Auschwitz? Would our shame be like that of the
Russian liberators insofar as it is the response of outsiders
who seem "oppressed . . . by a confused restraint which
seal[s] our mouths" and yet keeps our eyes fastened on the
"funereal scene"?

Before we look at Levi's elaboration, we should notice
that in the passage about the Russians noted above he points
out that the shame he is focusing on is the shame of a

particular type of person in a particular type of situation, "the shame which the just man experiences when confronted by a crime committed by another." This is the shame of the bystander, who, instead of doing something to prevent a crime or to interrupt it, allows the crime to occur and, Levi says, "feels remorse because of its existence." Here is a person who is himself just, who knows what is right and is the kind of person disposed to do it, and yet who allows a crime to occur, who, that is, fails to be himself, and in so doing allows something to be done, to exist, that is an affront to the just life and hence to his life. Levi calls this feeling of shame "remorse" and "guilt," but it is neither exactly. What is it?

Levi says that this shame as a kind of suffering was felt by the released prisoner "because of a reacquired consciousness of having been diminished." As he goes on to point out, the prisoner had "lived for months and years at an animal level"; his time had been filled with hunger, fear, and fatigue without "any space for reflection [or] reasoning." He had stolen, even from other inmates. At the time, in the camp, there may have been little opportunity to see oneself in this light, as living this way, but once the prisoner was released, there was time and opportunity to look at oneself as one had lived and become. Now clearly this is not true in the same way for the Russian liberator or for us today; what is relevant for us are the crimes or actions of others and our omissions or the omissions of those with whom we identify or who represent us. If the prisoner was diminished as a human being by having lived a certain way, then we, bystanders or heirs of bystanders, are diminished by having failed to act or by being the heirs and perhaps beneficiaries of such omissions. What is similar here is that shame requires a kind of detachment and the opportunity and capacity to enact it; it also involves the employment of that detached attention to look at the self and to see how its actions (or omissions) disclose a deficiency or inadequacy so that the self appears to itself as less than it expects itself to be.

The one ashamed feels under a kind of judgment, but for what?[19] For having done what one should not have done or for not having done what one should.[20] In Levi's case and for others who were in Auschwitz with him, he takes shame to have arisen, for some, precisely because they had not resisted; they had not done anything, or at least not all that they might have done, to oppose that which oppressed them.[21] Even if there was little reason to expect such resistance or little reason to think it could have been effective or even beneficial, there is the feeling that not resisting was inadequate and hence a judgment, one that the prisoner, afterwards, might recognize, is being made of him. He might think that he was not courageous enough, too weak, somehow too willing to sacrifice his dignity. Moreover, this judgment or accusation, as Levi calls it, might come from two directions, either from others or from oneself. And it is worse, he thinks, when it is self-accusation. But what does this mean?

One dimension of shame can be associated with the way others might look at us, and in this way the judgment upon us comes from outside. In the case of resistance, Levi remembers his account in *Survival in Auschwitz* of the hanging of a resistor before the assembled prisoners. As a survivor, he says, he believes that he sees a judgment "in the eyes of those (especially the young) who listen to his stories and judge with facile hindsight, or who perhaps feel cruelly repelled." The judgment is "you too could have [resisted], you too certainly should have [resisted]," and the survivor "feels accused and judged."[22] In such a way, the prisoner may feel shame in view of how others seem to be responding to his omission, but the shame can be mitigated, even if it is felt, by the thought that the judgment or accusation is misplaced, made "with facile hindsight" about how possible and reasonable resistance was. Levi sees here a shame that may be felt but that is unnecessary, in a sense, to the degree that the accusation is itself inappropriate.

But, he continues, "more realistic is self-accusation, or the accusation of having failed in terms of human solidarity." What Levi means is that "almost everybody feels guilty of having omitted to offer help" to another, of failing in basic human solidarity, failing to listen, to speak to another, to give even a "momentary attention" to the other's entreaty. Hence, the shame of self-accusation in such cases is the feeling of having failed to respond or reach out. It is not just a sense of having failed to be what others expect us to be; it is a sense of having failed to be what we expect of ourselves. Such shame is despair over who we are when we see ourselves as having omitted to do what we expect of ourselves. It does not require the "eyes" of the other judging us, real or imagined. The accusation comes from ourselves.

With these insights in mind, Levi tells a story of having found a small amount of water in Auschwitz at a time when thirst tortured the prisoners. Levi shared the water with his friend Alberto, but he was seen by Daniele, another prisoner, who later reminded Levi of his failure to share the water with him as well. Levi speaks of his shame at having failed to share the water with Daniele; while he is not sure whether that shame is justified, it does exist, he says, "concrete, heavy, perennial." There is, then, shame before another and shame before oneself; shame is a feeling of failure and inadequacy and having been diminished, but in one case it responds to the other's judgment, while in the other it is a response to one's own accusation. Whether some particular other person does or could judge our omission, or whether we judge ourselves, the shame we feel about ourselves marks our failure of human solidarity if what we omitted to do is to reach out when addressed by the other's entreaty, the other's imploring face.[23]

Levi recalls the incident of his failing to share the water with Daniele, and whether his self-accusation is justified or not, he admits to feeling ashamed. At the end of the chapter, he returns to this sense of having failed in human solidarity. "There is another, vaster shame," he says, "the shame of the world." Citing John Donne, he notes that we live together and are responsible one for another—"every bell tolls for everyone." Each of us is called to do what we can to care for the suffering and the hungry. Levi and his compatriots were swallowed by an "ocean of pain." Having lived in it together, they could not live as if alone. The just, he says, "felt remorse, shame, and pain for the misdeeds that others and not they had committed, and in which they felt involved." On the one hand, as we have seen, that shame was shame about themselves and their omissions. It was a sense of failure and of being diminished. But it was another kind of shame too, and this is the vaster shame that Levi has in mind here. He says it was grounded in the realization that "what had happened around them and in their presence, and in them, was irrevocable." That is, it was done and could not be undone; it could not be eradicated or washed away. Having been done, it was always a potential for humankind. Hence, Levi suggests, one feels ashamed at being human in such a human world. This, I take it, is what Levi means by the vaster shame, "the shame of the world." It is not a shame grounded in what one has done or in what one has omitted to do; it is a shame about being in a world in which such evil, pain, and suffering—such atrocities—exist and are a part of human potential.

In *The Drowned and the Saved*, Levi's reflections are largely about shame for what one has done or omitted to do, or, in the case of shame about the world, for what has been done in the world in which one lives. As I emphasized, Levi comments that shame may be more or less justified, more or less reasonable and grounded. We might say that some shame, based on what we have done or failed to do, is fitting and appropriate to who we are, while some shame is inappropriate, excessive, and perhaps even misplaced. I have in mind Levi's narrative of his own failure to share the water with Daniele and his comments about resistance. Levi seems to have been willing to say that shame about not striking a blow against one's oppressor is wholly misplaced, whereas shame about not listening to a fellow inmate, not acknowledging a look, or not speaking to another prisoner may well be justified even if it is not required.

Something analogous is the case with regard to shame that arises in a different way, and it is something that Levi refers to on several occasions in *Survival in Auschwitz*. Often we are ashamed of ourselves for looking the way we do, for having certain properties or features. It is often the case, for example, that in societies permeated with racial or ethnic bias, members of a group that is oppressed and belittled are ashamed of looking the way they do and of having certain features—hair of a specific texture or color, noses or eyes or lips of a certain shape—or of wearing certain clothes, of not having certain tastes or skills or abilities. In *Anti-Semite and Jew*, Jean-Paul Sartre argues that both the antisemite and the Jew can be inauthentic by measuring themselves by standards that are imposed by others and then by feeling ashamed or diminished precisely because they fail to meet those standards. Levi notices that the death camp inmate could feel such shame by looking a certain way and having certain features. When his training as a chemist gave him the opportunity to work in the camp laboratory, he was presented to the German doctors before he was selected to work there. Three young German girls worked in the laboratory. Levi reflects on how they looked at the inmates:

> Faced with the girls of the laboratory, we three feel ourselves sink into the ground from shame and embarrassment. We know what we look like: we see each other and sometimes we happen to see our reflection in a clean window. We are ridiculous and repugnant. Our cranium is bald on Monday, and covered by a short brownish mould by Saturday. We have a swollen and yellow face . . . our neck is long and knobbly. . . . Our clothes are incredibly dirty, stained by mud, grease, and blood.[24]

Earlier in *Survival in Auschwitz*, Levi spoke about his first experience in the laboratory, when he was interrogated by Dr. Pannwitz. Levi describes their encounter and especially Pannwitz's look:

> that look was not between two men; and if I had known how completely to explain the nature of that look, which came across as if across the glass window of an aquarium between two beings who live in different worlds, I would also have explained the essence of the great insanity of the third Germany.

The laboratory girls looked at Levi and his compatriots with repulsion, disdain, and humor; Pannwitz looked at him with utter detachment and an impression of carelessness. Levi remembers that he felt a "mad desire to disappear, not to take the test." This experience, I take it, is one of shame. Whether it is shame before the look of revulsion or shame before the look of lack of concern or solidarity or relatedness, it is shame, a sense of one's own unworthiness, of one's own repulsiveness, stench, and offensiveness. Levi took himself to be someone or something upon which no one should have to gaze, at which no one should have to look. One could serve others best by disappearing, by not being present. Shame is about self-negation.

But while there may be cases when such shame is warranted, when one is responsible for having put oneself in such a shameful—offensive or repulsive—state, there are times when one ought to be "ashamed" at being ashamed, when one's shame is itself mistaken and inappropriate.[25] The Jew's sense of shame when confronting antisemitic attitudes or practices, akin to what is known as Jewish self-hatred, is such a state. That shame is itself offensive, for it is an unwarranted, misplaced, and distorting feeling about oneself, and one about which one ought to be ashamed. Feeling ill about oneself for having features that one should not be ashamed of having, whether one has them or not, is itself worthy of shame. If shame is an emotional form of self-criticism about who one is, then it, like any criticism, can be well-taken or poorly formed and developed. Just as one can be unjustified in feeling shame about having failed to resist the Nazis, so one can be unjustified in feeling shame about how one looks to one's oppressors or to others or about how one feels about being taken by others as repulsive or inadequate, as cowardly or arrogant, as too shy or unassuming. And if one is unjustified and is persuaded by that fact, then one can feel ashamed at being ashamed or, alternatively, proud about—or at least accepting of—one's sense of shame.[26]

Were the three girls in the laboratory justified in treating the Auschwitz inmates as repulsive and disgusting? Did it make sense for Levi and the others to feel ashamed at how they looked and were taken to be? Levi's account uses two devices to suggest that the prisoners do look the way the girls view them and hence that their shame at looking that way is appropriate: they look at one another and even see themselves reflected in clean windows. Even if the prisoners can no longer smell the difference that their odor carries, they can look at others from a distance, in a detached way, and they can even see themselves as if in a mirror, reflected and facing them. When they do so, they can see how alien and repulsive they look, not by the girls' standards alone but even by their own. In the camp, they are normal and ordinary, but when measured against standards of everyday life, they are awful to look at, to smell, to be with. The girls' disdain makes sense and is justified, and hence their sense of shame about themselves makes sense. Or does it? After all, what are these standards? Why do they not apply in the camp? How is it that Levi looks and smells as he does? Is it shame he should feel or something else, perhaps anger, bitterness, or even pride?

RESPONSES TO SHAME ABOUT AND FOR THE WORLD

For Levi, there is something shameful about going on at all, after having been an inmate in Auschwitz along with so many others who were slaughtered or who died. He discusses the shame of having acted in certain ways, of having failed to act, of being degraded, and of now being alive at all as a privileged survivor—an undeserved privilege. He also points to the shame one feels as a survivor, or as a bystander, or as a German, as a Jew, as a human being alive in the world. One can feel shame, then, for those groups or in behalf of them, for Germans or for survivors or for all human beings. This last could be what he means when he talks about the vaster shame, the shame of the world; this might be a shame at being human at all in a world in which there was an Auschwitz and in which there seem to be no reliable obstacles to its repetitions.[27]

Let me suggest that it was this kind of shame that I felt as I watched *Ghosts of Rwanda*, as I read the memoirs of Roméo Dallaire, the field commander of the UN peace-keeping force in Rwanda in 1994, and studied the books that recount the events of those months and years with vivid and precise details about the genocidal massacres, the brutality and precision of the slaughter—books such as those by Gérard Prunier, Linda Melvern, Alain Destexhe, Michael Barnett, Philip Gourevitch, and Samantha Power. Dallaire may have felt guilt about not having completed his mission satisfactorily. American leaders such as Madeleine Albright and Bill Clinton may have expressed guilt at not having argued for intervention or acting to intervene when they had the power and authority to do so. But we inhabitants of the First World, who lived through those years and who live now in a world in which the lessons of Auschwitz have not been learned and indeed in which they have been ignored or rejected, cannot feel guilt in the way that powerful leaders may do. We should and can, nonetheless, feel shame—about being citizens of nations that did nothing or acted insufficiently to prevent recent genocides, about the collective inhumanity of all peoples and nations as expressed in the actions, inactions, and procedures of the United Nations, and perhaps most of all at being alive in a world containing Auschwitz and then the atrocities in Cambodia, Bosnia, Rwanda, and Darfur. We should and can, I believe, feel shame about living in a world where genocide is always possible and where its prevention is continually negotiable, where genocide is only one matter among many, very much capable of being ignored or permitted, where Auschwitz can be forgotten and where it can be denied that what happened in Rwanda, for example, was genocide.[28]

When thinking about such shame, remorse about oneself and one's world, an image comes to mind. In *Shoah*, Claude Lanzmann's epic film about the Holocaust, there is a powerful sequence when Lanzmann interviews the barber, Abraham Bomba, in an Israeli barbershop. Years before, in Treblinka, Bomba had been made to cut the hair of Jewish women just prior to their being sent to their death in that camp's gas chambers.[29] Lanzmann's questions urge Bomba to recall details—where did the barbers cut the women's hair, how many barbers were there, how long did this go on, how did you cut their hair, what did you cut with, were there mirrors, how did you feel when you saw the women naked, when you saw them with children? There is a very dramatic, painful moment, when Bomba recalls that he had no feeling, he felt dead, and then he tells Lanzmann that one day women from his home town of Czestochowa were led in, many of whom he knew, some of whom were neighbors and close friends. As he continues to cut the hair of the man in the Tel Aviv barber's chair, Bomba goes on to say,[30] "When they saw me, they started asking me, Abe this and Abe that—'What's going to happen to us?' What could you tell them? What could you tell?" Bomba's voice begins to crack; he begins to weep, as he says, "A friend of mine worked as a barber—he was a good barber in my hometown—when his wife and his sister came

into the gas chamber . . . I can't. It's too horrible. Please."
Lanzmann prods him to go on, he resists, but eventually he
continues:

> They tried to talk to [my friend] and the husband of his sister.
> They could not tell them this was the last time they stay alive,
> because behind them was the German Nazis, SS men, and
> they knew that if they said a word, not only the wife and the
> woman, who are dead already, but also they would share the
> same thing with them. In a way, they tried to do the best for
> them, with a second longer, a minute longer, just to hug them
> and kiss them, because they knew they would never see them
> again.[31]

Bomba's tears are driven by the memory of that episode, of
what he had done and not done, of the women who asked
him what was to happen to them, of his friend—was it a
friend or Abe Bomba himself?—being confronted by his wife
and sister in Treblinka, seeking to give them a last hug and
kiss, yet going on cutting the hair. He remembers Abe Bomba
and the others then, in Treblinka, and now, in Tel Aviv. Are
they tears of guilt? Of loss? Of shame? Perhaps they are tears
of all, but at least of shame, at having done what he did and
now of saying it out loud, of describing it and admitting it,
before Lanzmann and before all the movie's viewers, before
all of us. They are tears of shame about how to go on, while
one does go on, about who one is and what the world is.
Bomba's tears grip us and call out to us, summon us to
remember, not to forget, and to feel our shame along with
his.

Abe Bomba's tears of shame come in remembering. Mine
too—shame for what has been done in our world and shame
that comes with remembering a past that has been forgotten.

The shame we ought to feel in reading about Cambodia, Bosnia, Rwanda, and Darfur bears on our failure to act, to intervene, to take note, but our failure bears both on the victims of these genocides and on the forgetting of the past that itself bears on our—the world's and philosophy's—failure.

Levi's shame is recalled and yet, one can see, it is also present in the recollection itself. For Levi, there is shame in testifying to the past, the shame that comes with his recognition of having been spared, of having survived, and of not being in a position to testify accurately, of not being the one who should be testifying, the one who cannot remember.[32] The text that Levi recalls from his own book *The Reawakening*, cited earlier, tells of how the shame that Levi remembered and that the prisoners had felt was mirrored in the shame they saw in the eyes and the faces of their liberators. The Russian liberators of the camps were struck dumb; they did not speak, nor did they smile or greet the prisoners. They did not, could not face them, and Levi saw in their stares, their expressionlessness, the shame he had known in the presence of others in the camps.

But that shame, the shame of the liberators, did come with liberation; it was part of a process of opening the camps to view, clearing them, releasing and recovering the prisoners, and eventually obliterating the camps themselves. Shame then brought with it obliteration, for by obliterating the camps, one was also trying to obliterate the shame that came with witnessing them and their victims. In fact, it is true that shame seeks to nullify itself by negating what gives rise to it.[33] For us, Resnais says, that too easily means forgetting. We may seek to avoid shame or dispose of it by forgetting, by treating the past as dead and gone, by closing off the past from the present or, as *Night and Fog* shows us, by allowing the present to cover over, bury, or isolate it as though the past is in its own world and separate from ours.

In reality, however, the prisoners, the survivors of the camps, can really be liberated only if they are remembered; if not and if the past, their lives in the camps, is dead and gone, forgotten, then they are not free. As William Rothman points out, there is a moment in Night and Fog when the camera captures prisoners standing behind a barbed-wire fence, staring at their liberators and at the camera of the liberators. The narrator asks, "Are they free? Will life know them again?" These questions, Rothman comments, are not for the prisoners alone; "they are no less questions about the world, questions for the world. They are questions about, questions for, us."[34]

As viewers of Resnais' film, as viewers of the ghosts of Rwanda and readers of accounts of Cambodia, Bosnia, and Darfur, should we and can we feel a shame that compels us to remember these pasts, to restore them to reality, and to make "life know them again?" And what does that phrase mean? What is it for life to know the past again, the past of horror and atrocity, of brutality and genocide? What is it to "know" such pasts? If Rothman is right, part of such knowing is realizing that the fences of Night and Fog and the separation between image and reality, between past and present, are not real boundaries and barriers. To restore the reality of the past, to overcome forgetfulness, a failure to see and to understand, is to "acknowledge that—like the Kapo and the Nazi officer—this [prisoner who stares out at us in the film] belongs to our world, that we belong to his" and "the world of the film is our world." Realizing this, we can come to realize too that "responsibility for liberating the camps—condemning the executioners, laying the dead to rest, welcoming the survivors into our midst, freeing ourselves and our world—is in our hands, the hands of all us survivors."[35]

What can we expect of ourselves and our world? What might shame lead us to do? How might it lead us to live?[36] Levi comments that survivors are often asked whether Auschwitz could occur again, and while refusing to make judgments, he registers a few remarks. One is that Cambodia did occur, and he might have mentioned, had he lived today, Bosnia and Rwanda and Kosovo and now the Sudan. Another comment he makes is that mass slaughter is unlikely to occur in the Western world, Japan, and what was once the Soviet Union. Why not? Because, he says, "a sort of immunizational defense is at work which amply coincides with the shame of which I have spoken."[37] The ethnic cleansing in Bosnia and Kosovo belies Levi's hopes, but let me set aside that issue and ask what he meant when he spoke of shame coinciding with a sort of "immunizational defense." What did he have in mind?

Shame is about feeling unworthiness, for ourselves individually, for members of groups or nations of which we are members, and for humanity as a whole, for our world, as a place which does not measure up. Measure up to what? Charles Taylor has argued that shame is one of those emotions that requires a sense of import, of mattering, about certain properties or ways of life or actions. Such a sense of import is what I have tried to bring to attention in this chapter while commenting on Levi and his notion of judgment or accusation and when I used the word *standards*. Shame is how we feel about ourselves, our groups, and our world when they do not meet standards of worth and value. But what are the standards that figure into our shame at living in a world in which Auschwitz and subsequent genocides exist?

Just as the shame we feel has several dimensions, so are

there many standards against which our failures are measured. Levi refers to our sense of human solidarity. Others, such as the Holocaust survivor-philosopher Jean Améry, speak of our sense of solidarity with all those whose human dignity is under assault.[38] Some religious thinkers refer to a defense of the notion of being created in the divine image.[39] Perhaps no one has captured more profoundly than Emmanuel Levinas the preeminence of this sense of human sociability as fundamentally valuable for all human life and hence as that sense of human mutual responsibility which ought to determine how we live and all that we do. Genocide, the slaughter of human communities, massacres, and all the brutality and cruelty that are part of these acts are dramatic and momentous rejections of this value. Levinas saw this and frequently spoke out about it. In Resnais' terms, sociability calls for our responsibility to make a world in which life will know the victims and survivors of genocides again, in which life knows the past. It calls for us to be the liberators of the prisoners and victims of the past and in this way to liberate ourselves from shame and from the artifice of pretending, forgetting, and evasion. One standard of our failure, in our own eyes, is the standard of responsibility for the life and well-being of others, responsibility to care for the needy and to aid the suffering. Shame at failing to meet such a standard is what Levi saw in the speechless eyes of the Russian liberators.

But for us, watching reports about the Sudan today, reading accounts of the massacres in Rwanda and Srebrenica and Kosovo, the shame we might feel is also about the failure of forgetting, of allowing the past to be dead.[40] It is the shame about denial, specifically the denials of the leaders of the United Nations, of the United States, and of other countries— for example, Great Britain, France, Belgium—that what has occurred is genocide. Hence it is also shame about our having avoided an obligation to others, to ourselves, to all humankind. It is about carrying out a liberation of the victims of the past that is in effect a false liberation, a way of avoiding who we ought to be by cutting off the present from the past.

Shame, then, can accompany the failure of the wrong kind of liberation, but it can also lead to true liberation, to overcoming the forgetting, the avoidance, and the failure. Shame can lead to recovery of who we want ourselves to be, to a truer self.[41] Responding to shame this way, however, is no easy task; the shame itself, an iteration of Levi's shame and that of the Russian liberators, shows how deep and broad it can be, how resistant we are to an honest recovery of our selves and an honest confrontation with the demons of Auschwitz and genocide. Responsibility is not a speechless, immobilized response to the face of horror and atrocity but rather the word of kindness itself and the touch of care and concern, a living for others that is a more genuine way of living with ourselves. When shame gives rise to remembering, it breaks down barriers, and when the barriers come down, what stands before us, reaching out, is another person.[42]

Shame, then, can be a motivation for us to do what we can to oppose the forces of genocide in our world. We live in a world of extraordinary hunger and poverty, a world in which millions suffer at the hands of others, and a world in which neglect and self-indulgence risk the future of nature itself. It is also a world of ethnic cleansing and genocide. To these grave matters, we might respond emotionally in any number of ways, from worry to despair, from bitterness to anger, and from fear to anxiety. My proposal is that we elicit in ourselves shame regarding these actions, that this shame is one that we cultivate in order to unsettle and disturb ourselves, that it is an emotion we can and should share with our fellow citizens and with all humankind, and that it is an emotion that can, if properly confronted, lead to productive action to prevent such atrocities now and in the future.

Proposing such a response, however, may seem at best confusing, if not wholly impossible. Shame involves self-criticism based on how we are or seem to be as viewed by others; it is an emotional reaction and a very personal one, in which we focus our attention on ourselves and feel demeaned. How can we elicit such an emotion voluntarily and what makes it especially appropriate to do so in this kind of situation? And how can it be felt collectively, when it seems to be so private? And of what use is it to feel such shame, when it is so disturbing and would seem to immobilize us rather than lead to productive conduct? We need to say more about shame, it would seem, before this proposal can be taken seriously.

Two

I have provided the sketch of a narrative about *how we ought to react emotionally* to our situation in a world of suffering, atrocity and genocide, how cinema and literature may facilitate and complicate that emotional reaction, and finally how we ought to respond morally to that emotion. The name I have given to this emotional reaction is "shame," and when I first introduced it, I made some brief remarks about what shame is. But "shame" is a very complex and contested word, for several reasons, and in view of such complexity what I am recommending, as I have pointed out, may seem at least unclear and perhaps simply wrong. If shame is a spontaneous emotional response, how can we be persuaded to have it? If its self-criticism is global and imprecise, how can it be directed at a specific failure? If it is a self-conscious emotion, how can one have it in behalf of all humankind? And if it derives from standards or ideals that others apply to us, of what moral relevance is it to our own self-understanding and our own self-respect? In order to address questions such as these, we need to consider further the complex character of shame.[1]

THE COMPLEXITIES OF SHAME

First, insofar as "shame" refers to an emotional state, that emotion is sometimes experienced and acknowledged, and sometimes unacknowledged and hidden.[2] It has a phenomenology or what we might call experiential features, but that phenomenology is not always occurrent, so to speak. One of the implications of this characteristic of shame is that shame might be much more widely present in society than would seem to be the case from appearances. Surveys that ask participants to identify the emotion they have felt cannot count on the subjects' accurate identification of their shame. When asked about their feelings, subjects sometimes call them guilt, shame, disgrace, humiliation, and more. Moreover, as psychoanalytic accounts suggest, shame is often expressed in anger or rage and in despair or depression, as well as in other emotional or behavioral forms. If all of this is so, then shame will be harder to identify than one might have thought and its central features harder to isolate.

Second, the word "shame" might be taken to refer to an occurrent emotional state or alternatively to a tendency to react in certain ways, that is, as a dispositional, on-going state, what is sometimes called "shame-proneness." If what I am interested in is to motivate a moral response to atrocity and genocide, then the kind of shame I have in mind must be occurrent. Third, "shame" may be taken to refer to a cluster of emotional states or to one such state that can be elicited or produced by a variety of external conditions. That is, if one takes shame to be a feeling of failure or inadequacy, a desire to hide or conceal oneself from the view of others, a sense of distress or despair, and an anxiety about one's self or character as a whole, then it might be thought to be one emotion alongside others, like anger, that arises in us without any willfulness on our part, when certain conditions are present. Alternatively, if we take "shame" to refer to that emotional state together with a grasp of some standard or rule or ideal that we have failed to meet, a sense of being viewed critically by others in terms of our having failed that standard, and a self-reflective judgment about our very selves or character as a whole, then "shame" may be understood as one of a cluster of similar emotions and indeed itself as a family of emotions rather than a single one—akin to embarrassment, disgrace, humiliation, and guilt but different from all of them.

Fourth, shame might be treated as a prominent, even the dominant feature of our psychological lives, or it might be taken to be occasional and less pervasive. Freud came to treat guilt as our dominant emotion, and until recently much psychological literature supported that view. But in recent decades, shame has replaced guilt as the basic emotion of choice in social and psychological studies, particularly of Western societies. One reason for this change concerns the way guilt and shame are now frequently distinguished: guilt is thought to be focused on specific behavior or action, while shame is thought to be aimed globally at the whole self. When shame is viewed this way, it is taken to be more fundamental than guilt to the development and maintenance of one's overall identity; it is more pervasive than guilt as an expression of one's sense of having failed to be the person one wants to be. For this reason, shame is taken to be more fundamental. Another reason for such priority is that shame is associated with a set of increasingly urgent social problems, such as racial injustice, increased violence, women's rights and the rights of gays and lesbians, child abuse and the abuse of women, that characterize life in Western societies during the past several decades. Psychological studies of the so-called shame-rage spiral and the role of shame in the education of minorities have emphasized the ways in which socially aberrant behavior is grounded in the sense of personal inadequacy associated with humiliation, the loss of self-esteem, and shame.

Finally, philosophers have debated whether shame is an emotion with significant moral relevance or whether it is morally irrelevant and perhaps morally disadvantageous. It is widely agreed that the sense of distress or anxiety one feels with shame is somehow related to appearances, to how one looks to others or how one takes oneself to appear to others. To be sure, at the same time, shame concerns our sense of ourselves globally rather than our sense of having failed in the performance or non-performance of some particular bit of behavior. But it is often held that shame depends upon standards set for us by others. Hence, since shame is a reaction to having failed to meet a standard or rule or ideal, and since some philosophers take an emotion to be morally relevant only if it is grounded in the self's autonomous articulation of what is right or wrong, they argue that shame would be morally relevant only if it were autonomously grounded. Another way of putting this point is to say that guilt is essentially tied to moral notions such as responsibility, whereas shame is not.[3] But if it is a reaction to how others view us given standards grounded in those others, then how can shame be morally relevant? Some philosophers deny that it can be. Others argue that we need a more nuanced view of how the self and those other persons are related in terms of the standards or ideals that the self uses to judge itself, and such a nuanced view will redeem the moral worth of shame.[4] But even this strategy does not convince everyone. Shame is taken by some to be too oppressive and immobilizing to be morally valuable.[5] It may be self-protective, as has been claimed, but it is too imprecise and too overwhelming to be productively so. Shame does not tell us what to do to correct our faults, nor does it encourage a responsible effort to remove the sense of self-disgust or disgrace.[6] Moreover, to others shame seems too conservative to be morally beneficial, since it encourages the self to return to a kind of equilibrium or balance, even when the standard that has been transgressed or the ideal that one fails to meet is itself deserving of revision or rejection.[7]

These are some of the complexities that complicate any discussion of shame. To suggest, as I have, that shame would be an appropriate and useful emotional response to recent genocidal acts, to the cinematic and literary representations of them, and to the memory of the suffering and atrocity of the past half century, is to find ourselves immersed in this complexity. What exactly am I suggesting? What is shame? What is the special kind of shame I have in mind? Can one recommend shame as an emotional response for moral purposes? Is shame an emotion one can choose to have—or at least choose to acknowledge—and if it is, how is such shame unlike much that we call by that name?

MORALLY RELEVANT SHAME

Let me begin by noting a set of salient features of shame. Not every psychologist, sociologist, or philosopher who has discussed or examined shame would agree with all of these features, but in studies of shame they do crop up with enough regularity to have a certain credibility. To begin, shame has what I have called a phenomenology. That is, it does have an experienced quality about it; one feels a sense of distress or upset, uncomfortable and perhaps more than that.[8] One tends to look away from others, to want to hide, not to have to face some one or others in general.[9] Why? Because someone has said something calling attention to how we look or the way we talk or to something that we have done; or we have done something or failed to do something that affects others, some one or many others. That is, *something in us, really in us or only apparently in us, or something we have done or seem to have done, elicits in us a sense of distress about how we seem to us to be perceived by others, real or imagined.* Furthermore, we feel as we do because we have internalized the external judgment of failure or inadequacy. If we are thought to have a certain feature—facial or bodily—or a certain style or habit, we accept that we do and accept too the judgment that it is unworthy or a fault. We are distressed by the way our nose looks or our eyes, or we are disgusted by our obesity or by our facial physiognomy, or we find our way of speaking foolish or repulsive, and we do so precisely insofar as others judge (or would judge) it to be so and we accept their attitude toward that feature. Finally, in viewing ourselves as foolish or repulsive or inadequate or unworthy, we pass judgment on ourselves as a whole. This is what I have meant by calling shame "global." It is focused on *the self as a whole* even when it is elicited by a particular feature or action. That is, we view ourselves as inadequate or unworthy insofar as we are too tall or too obese or insofar as we speak in embarrassing ways or have acted badly by failing to help a friend or by making the choice we did. These, then, are the features that I want to call attention to: shame involves some kind of emotional reaction; it incorporates some sense of apparent failure; the failure involves losing face before others, actual others or imagined others; and it is a kind of self-criticism whereby the self charges itself with inadequacy overall, as the self that it is.[10]

My proposal is that we respond to living in a world of genocide with shame. But if the foregoing features of shame are the salient ones, can there be a form of shame that is morally significant, beneficial?[11] Must shame be a spontaneous reaction, or can we choose to be ashamed? And if we can, can we be ashamed not only of ourselves but, in a sense, of us all—that is, for us all? Moreover, can we be ashamed of something that we cannot on our own prevent? Clearly, the shame to which I am calling attention is not typical or characteristic. It is self-critical, to be sure, and unlike embarrassment, it is meant to be intense, sufficient to make us feel very uncomfortable and dissatisfied with who we are and how we act. Nor is it a feeling of humiliation that I am recommending, since one can only feel humiliated and diminished if something is done to us that leads to the feeling, and what I am recommending is that we call a feeling into being ourselves, given how we see our role in a certain situation.[12] In fact, the point of the emotion I am calling for, the shame, is not to expose ourselves to others in such a way that we seek to hide from them. Rather it is to attend to ourselves in such a way that we feel extreme discomfort with ourselves, perhaps to the degree that we want to conceal our failure from others but only insofar as we believe that others too should feel the same way. We feel, that is, a kind of collective desire not to confront each other in regard to a fault that we all share.[13] In view of such reflections, then, in what sense is this shame?

Let me side with those who take shame to be a normal feature of our lives. Chuck is ashamed about not being able to speak without stuttering; Doris is ashamed because she believes that her husband no longer finds her attractive and sexually desirable. Instances of shame like these occur regularly. We experience mild episodes of shame and more severe ones, some barely more than embarrassment and some very intense and persistent. Shame can become pathological, to be sure, when it debilitates us, leads to depression, and perhaps to acts of violent rage. Sometimes it is justified, when we have in fact failed to do something that is generally thought to be the right thing to do and take this as a taint on our character; sometimes it is unjustified, the result of racial or religious persecution. Nonetheless, shame is pervasive in our lives. If I call upon us to feel shame, I am not asking us to cultivate an exotic or strange emotion but rather one that is familiar.

Furthermore, shame is useful. Most of the time shame is self-corrective, as Gabriele Taylor claims, even if the correction it encourages is ultimately undesirable or itself unworthy. That is, shame is one of those emotions that is a check on what we do or who we are; it is a device for calling to our attention what might otherwise go unacknowledged. In response, we try to remove the shame or camouflage it—by blaming others or by sublimating it—or we capitulate to it and are overwhelmed. In short, shame is, at least at times, functional and adaptive. Shame helps us to grow and develop, and it assists us in our social relationships, our relationships with others. Even when it is unjustified, when a wife is ashamed about giving up a career when she chooses, after deliberation and reflection, to stay at home and parent her children, or when a minority student is shamed into thinking that he is worthless and incapable by teachers who demean him and treat him with virtual contempt, shame can be useful—by warning us that we are subject to an external criticism that we have accepted and internalized and that we should consider seriously the justification and the truth of that criticism.[14]

As psychologists have noted, shame is a jolt or shock, which pulls us up short and immobilizes us. Emotionally, that is, shame provokes reflection and self-examination, both in order to assess who we are and in order to assess our relationships with certain others. I want to capitalize on this aspect of shame, its capacity to destabilize us and call us to attention. Here is an emotion with which we are familiar and which pervades our lives. In its natural forms, when it arises spontaneously, it is responsive to a combination of situational factors—the existence of standards or ideals, the real or imagined criticism of others for failing those ideals, and our personal appropriation of that criticism. But in its artificial form, as we might call it, we can to some degree control what those standards or ideals are and who the others are. We can tell ourselves to feel shame; we can cultivate it, when we believe that we need to be jolted from our lethargy, when our moral inertia needs to be interrupted. In such a case, we do not simply react to circumstances and the judgment of others with a sense of regret or disgust with ourselves. Rather we orchestrate such a reaction in order to dislocate ourselves and disturb our indifference, our inattentiveness. What we seek is a motivation to self-evaluation and change and a revision of our relationships with others, and we use this emotion, because of its structure and its phenomenological texture, to facilitate this process.

There are risks to such a moral strategy. Emotions have a certain character, and shame is no different. It is painful to feel shame, disturbing and unsettling. Moreover, it involves a global sense of inadequacy and regret. As its detractors emphasize, it is for reasons like this that shame is considered a poor state in which to find oneself immersed. It is not fine-grained enough, or sufficiently focused, to motivate us to do what is needed to rectify or repair ourselves. In part, as I have mentioned, shame's deficiencies are associated with its imprecise target; unlike guilt, which is elicited by and targeted at a specific bit of behavior or a precise action, shame has an other-directedness about it, is itself less precise as a feeling, and targets the self as a whole rather than a discrete action. Given such features, then, shame can function as a warning or as a sign of real or imagined failure, but it can do so only at the risk of providing little assistance in rectifying the problem and even more worrisome, at the risk of leading to even worse behavior. As psychological studies have shown, and as I have mentioned, shame regularly leads to anger or depression. And the anger can itself generate further anger, or rage, eventuating in what has been called, following the pioneering work of the psychologist Helen Lewis, the shame-rage spiral. Shame can also provoke the self to a kind of avoidance, by blaming others for precisely the conduct or features that the self takes itself to lack or for the faults the self admits to having. In short, to provoke shame in oneself runs the multiple risks of responses of denial, of increasingly hostile behavior, or of immobilizing despair or depression. These are all among the normal and pathological responses to shame that are found in everyday life, and there is every reason to think that they are just as possible when the feeling of shame is artificially produced as they are when it comes naturally and spontaneously.

But the risks are worth taking. The escalation of acts of violence on a mass scale during the past half-century—from state sponsored genocides and ethnic cleansing to tribal massacres and the rampant slaughter of millions in the name of hostile ideologies—so dominate our world that nothing less than a resurgence of moral responsibility can hope to alter the situation.[15] We are presented with evidence of atrocities and suffering on such a great scale and with such frequency that our moral sensibilities are dulled and overwhelmed. Many do respond with assistance, but most of us have become indifferent. We ignore the suffering; we excuse ourselves and our political leadership; we accept the dictates of political and economic realism. We find ways to insulate ourselves from caring sufficiently both about those who suffer and about ourselves as the kind of people who do not commit ourselves to reducing that suffering. Among the emotional responses that one might cultivate in order to motivate in us a revision of our moral sensibilities and of our actions, shame is powerful enough to unsettle us and disturb us, even if it is a blunt tool, so to speak, rather than a precise technology.

WHY SHAME AND NOT GUILT?

But why not guilt? Why call upon ourselves to feel shame and not guilt? If we need a powerful emotional motivation to call attention to our faults and to elicit renewal and revision, why not turn to guilt?[16] In everyday experience, we have trouble distinguishing shame from guilt; we cannot be counted upon to see clearly how one emotion differs from the other. But psychologists and others who have studied these emotions do distinguish shame from guilt, conceived in terms of paradigm cases, in several ways. Helen Lewis, in her classic study of shame and pathology, emphasized, as we have earlier, that guilt is focused on specific bits of behavior or precise actions, while shame is aimed at the self as a whole, globally. This way of distinguishing the two has been adopted by many subsequent students of these emotions.[17] But even here we must be careful. Shame about one's height or weight or speech impediment are clearly not about what is in our control. Let us set such cases aside. There are cases where shame, like guilt, can be elicited by a specific transgression or a particular omission, that is, failing to keep a promise or failing to provide assistance or failing to respond to a request. But guilt not only starts with such an action; it also ends with it, in the sense that guilt is the feeling of failure one has when one judges that one's action or failure to act is wrong and that one is responsible and liable as the agent. Shame, on the other hand, may begin with a specific failure—although it need not, of course, but it never ends with that specific failure. Rather shame is a feeling of unworthiness that focuses on the self or on one's character or identity as a whole. As it is sometimes put, we feel guilty about what we have done; we feel ashamed about who we are.

But guilt and shame differ in other ways as well. The feeling of guilt lacks the social dimension that shame requires. Philosophers like to say that a relationship with others is required for shame. But we need to be clear about exactly how the other person figures into the experience of shame. Both guilt and shame are concerned with feeling unworthy or inadequate with respect to some standard or rule or ideal, of having failed to measure up, so to speak. When we feel guilt, we feel failure about having met a standard that can originate anywhere but that we ourselves accept. When we feel shame, we experience the pain of inadequacy both in the eyes of others or before others—we do not want to face them or cannot bear to look them in the eye—and in our own estimate. Here too there are standards or rules or ideals that we fail to measure up to, and here too we accept those standards as our own, but our accepting them is somehow tied to others' holding them and assessing us in terms of them. Psychologists are not at all clear about how these two aspects of shame are related—our own appropriation of certain standards or ideals and others' holding them and evaluating us in terms of them; nor are philosophers. Confusion or unclarity about this issue has bedeviled philosophical discussion about shame, and especially attempts to criticize shame as morally irrelevant and attempts to apologize for it and its moral significance.

Exactly how does shame require another person or other persons? Psychologists use various phrases or expressions as indications that a respondent to a survey or to questioning is referring to shame: did you feel that you wanted to hide from others? Did you look down or away from others? Did you feel that you lost face and were embarrassed? Of course, one could argue that treating these phrases and expressions and responses as indications of shame simply begs the question. But I think that most of us would agree that they do express our general sense that shame is a feeling we have about how we see ourselves *in terms of how others see us*. There might be actual other persons or a real other person who has said something to us or who looks at us in a certain way, or there may be no actual persons but rather our own sense of what we imagine others do or would say or how they do or would see us. This is what I meant earlier, in chapter 1, when I said that shame requires others, but they need not be actual others. We are being judged, or we imagine that we are being judged, but the crucial consideration is that we feel shame only when there is such other-judging of us. But, once again, as in the case of what conditions elicit shame and guilt, shame may proceed through this other-judging, but it does not end with it. Guilt, on the other hand, never proceeds through it. There is no such "stage" in feeling guilt; guilt does not pass through others, real or imagined. Guilt begins within ourselves and stays there; shame begins with others and then is internalized or passes into the self.

Noting this fact, that feeling shame requires turning to ourselves through other-judgment, real or imagined, may be sufficient to distinguish shame from guilt. But, as I pointed out, neither psychologists nor philosophers are generally very precise about how the other-judging of ourselves and the later stage of our self-judging of ourselves are related to one another.[18] Philosophers have been concerned about this relationship insofar as it contributes to a claim about the autonomy of the standards that the self applies to itself in judging itself to be inadequate or unworthy. That is, philosophers have been inclined to say that shame is morally relevant only if the standards it applies to itself come from itself and not from the other. This is a very Kantian framework within which to assess the moral relevance of shame; it assumes that shame can be a moral emotion only if it is, in some sense, autonomous and not heteronomous. But one of the unfortunate features of this strategy, aside from its implausibility as a measure of shame's moral relevance, is that it threatens to make shame a kind of emotional redundancy. If ultimately the self must accept certain standards or ideals on its own terms and as grounded in its own judgment, then the fact that others also hold those principles or standards is irrelevant, morally speaking. And if so, then shame appears to be a wholly unnecessary emotion, or at least the fact that it is associated with the judgment of others, real or imagined, seems to be unnecessary to it. The philosopher Bernard Williams tries to avoid this kind of problem by giving the other a significant status for the self, by restricting shame to cases where the self has sufficient respect for the other as a moral judge.[19] But while this might be true for certain cultures and societies, it is hardly true of our own, especially those cases of shame associated with racial persecution, the oppression of women, child abuse, and drug use, where either that respect does not exist or should not exist and yet where shame is rampant. What, then, is the relationship between the judging of the subject by some other or others, real or imagined, and the self's judging of itself?

First, there is a causal connection of some kind. That is, shame arises when we have feelings of inadequacy and distress about ourselves *because* others see us as flawed or unworthy. Shame is self-directed; it is shame about ourselves. But it is, in a sense, reflected distress; we feel discomfort because others judge us as inadequate. But this is not sufficient. The connection is more than causal. We also adopt the standards that the others use; we take our action to have been unworthy or our inaction to be disturbing, or we take our facial characteristics to be degrading or disgusting or repulsive. Moreover, we acquire the standard for judging ourselves from the others who do so or whom we take to do so. In addition, because we take their standards and agree that they apply, we feel repulsive *in their eyes*, so to speak. That is, we take ourselves to be inadequate both to ourselves and to them. Hence, we want to hide—from them and from ourselves. We are ashamed *about ourselves* but *before others*. Our relationship with others, then, is present in shame in several ways: it generates our self-judgment; it contributes the standards for it; and it is in a sense part of the judgment itself. This last feature is what one might call "exposure." That is, shame is not only about being inadequate or being a failure; it is not only about being an unworthy person, a failed self. It is also about being an *exposed* failed self, one that appears to others who think poorly of it and from whom it wants to hide or flee.

Guilt is not only about particular actions; it is also about taking responsibility for them and being able to admit that responsibility, to ask forgiveness, and to compensate for the failure. Shame is harder to deal with. Since other persons are involved, shame is less within our control in one sense, but in another there is more for us to be in control of. Let me explain. Shame makes us feel uncomfortable and in distress. What can we do to relieve it? We can, of course, as psychologists and psychotherapists tell us, feel depressed; we can blame others for the shame; we can accept the judgment and seek to correct the flaw; and so forth. Broadly speaking, we can consider the standards which others use and which we have adopted and evaluate them and our conformity with them. Alternatively, we can consider our relationships with others, real and imagined, in order to evaluate mutual influence, priorities, and more. Can we avoid shame? Not totally, of course, since most often it comes over us, like a wave, unavoidably. But we can do what we can to make it less likely to occur and to interrupt it, once we feel it. If removing guilt is about reconsidering standards that we use to judge ourselves and to correct our behavior in their light, as well as to compensate for past transgressions, then shame is complicated especially by the complex and multifaceted role that others play in it. There is less in our control overall, but, as I said, more is in the control that we do have.

I have been discussing how shame differs from guilt in order to clarify why my proposal is that we feel shame about living in a world of genocide. But the differences between standard shame and guilt may be helpful in ways that would not apply to the "voluntary" shame that I am recommending.

How much of this account applies to what I have called artificial shame? And does it help to explain why shame, rather than guilt, is better suited for us to use to motivate a morally responsible response to violence and suffering in the world we live in? There are three features of shame that make it attractive: (i) the fact that it eventually becomes a form of self-criticism in a global sense, a self-criticism of the self as a

whole and not restrictedly of one aspect of the self or one
action that has been performed, and has a serious depth to it;
(ii) its intensity and capacity to unsettle and disturb us; and
(iii) the way that it has both personal and collective dimensions. Despite its deficiencies or problems, then, shame is an
appropriate moral emotion to call upon in this situation. Let
me say something about each of these attractions.

Shame runs deep, and part of this depth is that it reaches to
who we are overall, the kind of persons we are. To be sure,
this depth is in part a function of how serious the issue is that
gives rise to the shame or at least how serious it seems. One
can be mildly shamed, when our sense of discomfort is very
much like embarrassment, but one can also feel seriously
ashamed, utterly disgraced or humiliated, when the discomfort is overwhelming and barely endurable. But whatever the
issue that elicits it or the degree of its intensity, all shame is
about our overall character and not about the specific feature
or action in question. And that fact, its reach to the self, makes
it a very serious and deep matter. Hence, when the issue is in
fact a serious one, as the issue of violence, atrocity, and genocide is, to awaken us from our moral lethargy one should call
upon a deep emotion, and shame fits the bill in this regard.
And unlike guilt, shame is about the self and not in a limited
way about something specific that one has done. Since I am
not recommending that we react emotionally in order to feel
motivated to perform some antecedently determined action
and since our goal is future conduct that will contribute to
preventing genocide or intervening to stop it, shame is more
appropriate than guilt.

Intensity of emotion, moreover, runs to force as well as
depth. That is, the more intense the emotion, the greater its
capacity to disturb us and unsettle us. This is not always true,

of course; some powerful emotions may solidify us in existing patterns of behavior and in existing attitudes. Nor is it always salutary. Some powerful emotions may disturb us to the point of pathology and neurosis; not all are going to be beneficial. But, as we indicated above, if the issues are serious enough and the strategies of denial or indifference powerful enough, then strong emotions are called for, and shame certainly can be one. Guilt, anger, and fear can also be very intense, and we would not want to deny that they can be. My point, however, is that shame can also be intense and unsettling in similar ways.

Finally, the shame I have in mind would incorporate a feeling of unworthiness and self-reproach targeted at us as part of Western society and indeed of all humanity. Part of what I mean is that each of us would feel ashamed in the face of others; it ought to be an emotion that holds all of us in its grasp. Moreover, it is acknowledgment of fault of a collective kind. Hence, it is shame *for us all about us all* and about each of us in the face of each and every other. Since it is not targeted at a single action or omission but rather at an overall situation of insufficient attention and action, guilt is not appropriate. Nor is guilt, technically speaking, possible here, since the emotion here is collective in a complex sense. To be sure, Karl Jaspers, in *The Question of German Guilt*, does refer to what he calls "metaphysical guilt," a kind of guilt for all humankind for the Nazi genocide as part of the human world itself. But Jaspers' discussion of guilt was focused on Germans and hence on perpetrators of the Nazi atrocities and those who by association might be implicated in them. Since I am dealing with people throughout the world who are, in a sense, bystanders, I think that this emotion is better conceived as a form of shame. Hence, what I have in mind is something similar, a shame for all humankind insofar as the human world contains and continues to contain a vast array of horrors of suffering and atrocity.[20] Focused on the Holocaust and the Nazi genocide and on their agents, Jaspers' terminology may be appropriate, but expanded as I suggest, guilt is no longer suitable. Shame is more fitting, even with its flaws.

But, one might object, how can we feel shame, even collectively, about something that each of us was powerless to prevent in the past and is powerless to prevent in the future? I have claimed that one can feel an emotion personally and yet share that emotion with others, and in the case of shame, one can share it with the very people before whom one feels ashamed. The objection cannot be, then, that shame seems inappropriate in cases where we collectively are powerless to prevent the actions which have given rise to our shame. For surely there is reason to think that collectively all of humankind could, in principle, create conditions in which genocides would not occur; if a world free of genocide and such atrocities is a worthy ideal, it is a collective one. The objection, then, must be that shame seems pointless for each of us personally with regard to such large-scale events which we are powerless to prevent.

Here we need to distinguish between two modes of change that shame calls for. On the one hand, shame calls our attention to a characteristic we have or are perceived as having or an action we have performed or are taken to have performed, and we can seek to alter that characteristic or compensate for that action.[21] Suppose, for example, that we are made to feel ashamed of our weight or the clothes we wear. If so, we can choose to do something about these matters, if we take the judgment seriously that gave rise to our feeling ashamed. Of course, even here the role of the shame is not a simple one.

The point of the shame is not necessarily to motivate us to change ourselves to meet the standards others set for us. If the flaw is one that we believe, on reflection, is a genuine one, then the point of the shame may indeed be to help us see that we need to alter ourselves. But if the flaw is not genuine, reflecting on the shame should reveal to us something about our relationships with others and our dependency upon them and their judgments.

On the other hand, shame does include a self-assessment about ourselves, and we can choose to change ourselves in some fundamental way or alternatively we can learn, by reflecting on the shame and the judgment of others that contributes to it, to alter our relationships with others, to deal with the judgments of others in a different way, and to look at ourselves differently. In short, shame can lead us to change the circumstances that gave rise to it, or it can lead us to change ourselves in some fundamental way.

Using these terms, in the case of collective shame, such as the kind I am recommending, the point of the shame is to do both. It is to motivate us to change both ourselves and the world in which we live. The shame should motivate us to reflect on the suffering and pain that genocides have caused and on the complicity of especially the affluent nations of the world in such horrors. As a result, we can individually change ourselves into persons who care and invest ourselves in contributing to the prevention of atrocity and genocide. Moreover, we can contribute to changing the world by collectively calling upon our leaders and others to make the most effective decisions aimed at preventing genocide and the systematic slaughter of innocent people.

Is shame not too immobilizing? Not necessarily. Others have recognized that there are episodes or kinds of shame that can be beneficial. The philosopher Gabriele Taylor, for example, distinguishes "false" from "genuine" shame, and whether one accepts this classification of natural or everyday feelings of shame, I would certainly want to claim that the kind of shame I have in mind is "genuine" insofar as it would focus our attention on our real failures, as humanity, in the face of standards or ideals of justice and mutual concern that are worthy of reconsideration. Robert Metcalf notes that Plato, in the *Crito* and in the *Symposium*, distinguishes bad from good shame, when he has Socrates argue in the former and has Alcibiades in the latter point to the fact that shame should be focused on the right person and the true standard of conduct. Moreover, while some have claimed that shame in general helps people avoid wrongdoing and failure, the psychologists June Tangney and Ronda Dearing do not find empirical support for this moral role.[22] They do, however, make a very interesting point:

> The acute pin of shame may in some cases motivate productive soul-searching and revisions of one's priorities and values. The challenge is to engage in such introspection and self-repair without becoming sidetracked by defensive reactions. . . . Such a positive function of shame might ensue from private, self-generated experiences of shame as opposed to public, other-generated shame episodes. Perhaps non-shame-prone, high-ego-strength individuals with a solid sense of self may occasionally use shame constructively in the privacy of their own thoughts.[23]

This is an important insight, as an empirical suggestion, that may provide some reason for accepting my proposal about eliciting shame as a vehicle for responding morally to geno-cides, massacres, and violence in our world.

If shame can be used productively, however, is it plausible to conceive of it as a collective emotion? Surely, feelings are had by each of us individually, but the interpersonal character of shame opens up for it the possibility that shame can link us together in what we might call a "web of interlocking shame" or a "community of shame," whereby each of us feels shame before all others, for what we collectively have become. I cannot explain how this occurs, but I sense an appreciation of this shift from personal to collective shame in a remarkable essay by James Agee, written in 1943 and only recently dis-covered among his poetry manuscripts.

In "America, Look at Your Shame!", Agee reflects upon an experience he had in 1943. Agee recalls seeing a photograph of two young white men, during the Detroit race riots, hold-ing up a bleeding black man, and staring at the camera with a kind of horror and selflessness, what Agee calls "a terrific, accidental look of bearing testimony." They were, he says, the kind of men he would have maligned as weak and senti-mental. Yet, seeing them in the photo, he says: "It made me ashamed of every such reflex of easy classification and dis-missal as I have ever felt—the more ashamed, because I had to wonder, whether, in such a situation, I would have been capable of that self-forgetfulness and courage." Later that afternoon, Agee found himself with some soldiers and sailors on a bus, obviously from the South as Agee himself was, mal-igning blacks, and he recalls his fantasies about courageously confronting them for failing to realize what the war against Hitler was all about and being beaten. But in fact they were only fantasies, "all so much cotton-batting on my tongue." He did not do anything. But an old black woman did:

> She was talking very little, and crying a little, and telling [one
> sailor], and the whole bus, that he ought to be ashamed,
> talking that way. People never done him no harm. Ain't your
> skin that make the difference, it's how you feel inside. Just
> might bout's well be Hitluh, as a white man from the South.
> Wearing a sailor's uniform. Fighting for your country. Ought to
> be ashamed.

Then Agee says: "I remembered the photograph in PM, and looked sternly at the floor, with my cheek twitching." That night he told the story to some friends and reports that the telling of it

> embarrassed me a good deal, but not as painfully as I wish it
> might have, and I found their agreement that they would have
> done the same almost as revolting as my own performance in
> the doing of it, and in the telling. So now I am telling it to you.

In this essay Agee exposes the sense of self-torment that comes with deep shame about who one is and what one wants to do but does not or perhaps cannot.[24] There is a movement, in Agee's reactions, from a personal sense of self-reproach to a sense of collective self-criticism, a multiplication of shame upon shame that focuses in the end on a charge to his readers, to feel that same shame about racism in America and America's failure of courage when confronted with it.[25]

I presented in chapter 1 an account of a process that led me to feel shame about the kind of world we live in—a world of genocide, atrocity, and suffering, and to feel shame about Rwanda, Darfur and other acts of genocide, and about our forgetting Auschwitz and all it means about suffering and inhumanity. One implication of that account is that arriving at such a sense of shame would be an important step. Shame is itself a response, but as I will elaborate in chapter 4 it also produces further responses. According to the psychologist Michael Lewis and many others, psychologically shame if unacknowledged registers in emotional substitution, depression or rage. In a sense, governments of the world and peoples, especially European nations, the United States, and the United Nations, failing to acknowledge shame for permitting such acts to occur, substitute such responses, anger and rage—excuses, justifications, and more—even criticism of the victims.[26] My point here is therapeutic; to deal with shame, one must first acknowledge it (Lewis calls this "owning the shame") and then understand the global character of shame in this new way. One must also understand what the failure is that has led to the shame and who is responsible for it—that is, it is not abuse or humiliation but rather justified shame. James Agee, for example, assumed the truth of racism in America. We deserve to be ashamed, he implied, for it is we who have contributed to that racism by failing in precisely the ways we are so inclined to avoid acknowledging.

The first commercial film on the Rwandan genocide, *Hotel Rwanda*, although it is a melodrama of a kind, a love story, and a story of heroism, does recall the genocide with some sense of accuracy and realism. With regard to the way in which shame can be used, there is one moment of special interest. When the French come to the Hotel, the guests expect that they are about to be saved. But the French soldiers loaded all the whites on the buses and left—in the rain. In the course of the evacuation, a Hutu lieutenant and soldiers appear in Paul Rusesabagina's bedroom, announcing that the Hotel will be evacuated. Paul rushes downstairs and fakes an old guest-list. The lieutenant is enraged. Paul calls the Sabena offices in

Belgium. He speaks to a shocked Sabena president, who eventually intercedes with the French president's office to save the Hotel and its occupants. But no one will return—not the Belgians, the French, the British, or the Americans—to protect them or to save them. Abandoned, Paul gathers the refugees and calls upon them to phone powerful and influential friends. He says:

> Say goodbye. But when you say goodbye, say it as though you are reaching through the phone and holding their hand. Let them know that if they let go of that hand . . . you will die. We must shame them into sending help . . .

It is a striking moment, of the failure and rejection of those on the outside, and testimony to the greatest weapon the refugees seem to have—the capacity to "shame" their friends into action. It is shame for inaction before those who will be the victims of that inaction; it is a shame based on deep assumptions about friendship and self-respect.[27]

As I have mentioned, psychologists since Helen Lewis have spoken of a shame-rage spiral. Shame can generate violence, which in turn can produce shame and then more violence, without end. Can we not speak too of a failure-of-shame/shame spiral? Suppose we fail to remember the horrors of the Holocaust, the suffering of Bosnia, of Cambodia, the massacres of Rwanda, and the slaughter and famine in Darfur. Should we not be ashamed? And if we are not, will not our children and grandchildren be ashamed of us, and will that shame not lead itself to a refusal to remember and hence a refusal to feel shame, which in its turn will become, in the generations thereafter a feeling of shame? In a poem, "*Shemá,*" based on the motifs of the Jewish affirmation from Deuteronomy 6:4, Primo Levi warns us of such a future. The poet calls attention to the victims of the Holocaust and their suffering, challenging us, "You who live secure/ In your warm houses . . ." to

> Consider whether this is a man,
> Who labours in the mud
> Who knows no peace
> Who fights for a crust of bread
> Who dies at a yes or a no.
> Consider whether this is a woman,
> Without hair or name
> With no more strength to remember
> Eyes empty and womb cold
> As a frog in winter.

He then calls us to "Consider that this has been . . ." and to "Repeat them to your children." The poem ends with the caution that if one does not follow these commands, the consequences may be dire: "Or may your house crumble,/ Disease render you powerless,/ Your offspring avert their faces from you." It is the last line that is the salient warning: remember, for if you do not, your children will be ashamed of you; they will seek to hide from you and turn away from you.[28] One should be ashamed lest one forget and fail to pass on the tale. Shame, then, is not only a motivation for self-criticism and a revised response to what has elicited it. It may also contribute to preventing its own return in the generations to come, for one can be ashamed of others with whom one identifies as well as ashamed before others whose judgment one takes seriously, before one's parents and grandparents.

Three

Most of us are not direct witnesses to the mass slaughter, the genocides, and the ethnic cleansing that have occurred during the past century. What we know of such events is mediated—by memoirs and testimony, by news reports, by fictional narratives, by photographs and now digital images, and by cinematic portrayals. If we are to feel shame about who we are and about our national character and about humankind, what elicits such shame would not be the events themselves, nor direct reproach in the eyes of others; such conditions are mediated by these modes of communication. About these too, I want to suggest, we can feel many things— saddened, angry, frightened, horrified, and also ashamed.[1]

A natural response to television news footage of atrocities and to photographs in newspapers and magazines is a sense of shock and then anger—aimed at the agents of brutality and massacre and then at our governments for participating in it or allowing it to continue. Why, then, have I chosen to focus on the way that shame can arise for us as readers of literature and viewers of films that represent genocide and mass killing? I have two reasons. The first is that I want to show how this kind of shame can deepen the shame we feel with regard to the events themselves. That is, I want to show how shame can be complicated and multi-dimensional. The second reason is that I want to focus on how shame can motivate us to reflect upon and change who we are; as I have pointed out, shame is a mode of self-criticism. My interest in literature and film, then, is not so much their role—like that of television, the news media, and such—in motivating public opinion. It is rather their role in leading us to self-reflection and self-examination, and then to a practical response that is based on an altered sense of who we are. Shame is one possible response to the depictions of atrocity and suffering, and unlike anger, shock, and revulsion, it is a response that we can employ for moral reasons as part of the task of education and self-assessment.

The atrocities and horrors of the twentieth and the early twenty-first centuries have not been discrete occurrences. Each is embedded in various historical narratives, and together these events are linked in many ways.[2] Auschwitz, the Nazi death camps, and the genocidal assault on Jews, Gypsies, and others, are bound up in memory with many subsequent atrocities—Cambodia, Bosnia, Kosovo, Rwanda, and Darfur among them. Furthermore, artistic imagination has sought to represent these events in various ways, and these too—cinematic and literary representations among them—regularly link the events to one another. If indeed one can and should feel shame about these events and ourselves in response to them, then that shame is ramified by their interrelations in our memories and in our representations. Moreover, the representations themselves can generate additional shame, elicited by inaccuracies or distortions or improprieties, that only intensifies and complicates the shame we might initially have felt. This chapter is about this latter phenomenon—the way in which cinematic and literary representations of the Holocaust and other genocides can have such effects on our emotional lives.[3]

Hence, here I propose to extend a thought introduced in the first chapter, and that concerns the representation of genocide and atrocity in literature and film. Earlier I showed how our shame, when confronted with evidence of recent genocides and atrocities, can be complicated by our awareness of humanity's failures with regard to earlier such events, for example, how our response to Bosnia, Rwanda, or Darfur can be ramified by our response to the Nazi Holocaust. Furthermore, our shame can be elicited by representations of recent genocides in literature and film. But that shame can be further complicated and ramified by those representations themselves when they themselves deny, compromise, or distort the events themselves. Of course, fiction and films can achieve a serious level of genuineness in one regard while failing in others; both are complex and multi-layered types of works. But they do not succeed in every regard, and when they fail, we can be ashamed because of the atrocities, and we can also be ashamed because of accounts and films of them. Our initial self-reproach can be complicated by a sense that we live in a world of distortion and mendacity and more.

SHAME AND REPRESENTATION

To begin, the shame I am going to be talking about in this chapter is a feeling or reaction that one might feel as a member of the audience of films and a reader of literature about the atrocities of the century. A film or novel may portray a character who experiences and lives with shame, but it can also seek to elicit a sense of self-reproach and self-criticism on the part of its audience. Both represented and elicited shame may be important to consider. Moreover, if one feels shame with regard to the event and remembering it, that shame can become intertwined with the shame that comes from watching a film about it or reading a novel or story about it, when those works do in fact evoke shame. But how might such shame occur and why?

Perhaps no formula can capture what I have in mind, but here is an example. In an essay by Stanley Cavell in his book of essays *Philosophy the Day after Tomorrow*, there is a remarkable account of Fred Astaire and a dance routine of his in a late movie, *The Bandwagon* (1953). The number, as Cavell interprets it, expresses Astaire's reflection on his indebtedness to black dance, his attempt to acknowledge and give praise to those to whom he is indebted, and to conceive an America, a Utopia, in which the owners of that tradition do not suffer the injustices of the America that has exploited them. Astaire's dance number, Cavell says, is all this and also a kind of rebuke and one that calls for something on our part, an apology perhaps.[4] What I draw from it, however, is that if the rebuke takes hold, then we viewers should feel a sense of shame in watching the number, given Cavell's reading of it, as inheritors of the America that has lived from that exploitation and profited from, indeed continues to profit from it. We could respond with a sense of shame, but it is likely we will not. We will work to avoid such an acknowledgment of fault together with the expression of hope and optimism that it might bring forth, in part through what Levinas calls "the temptation of theodicy," by explaining away, but also, as in this case, by watching a rebuke and an acknowledgment and yet not responding to it as a rebuke. It is a chastening thought, remarkable and painful. Watching the dance routine, after reading Cavell, one might feel doubly ashamed—ashamed of oneself for America and yet ashamed at avoiding the shame of America, at not responding, or at occluding the shame and its point.[5]

This is one example of how shame can be implicated in film. A cinematic or literary representation can be an explicit rebuke or a more subtle one, and when it is either, that rebuke might very well elicit shame in us, the viewers or readers. Alternatively, it may be that a work intends or provides no reproach but in a sense is a reproach, because of the way that it represents or misrepresents what it calls to mind.

In chapter 1, I called attention to *Night and Fog* and the documentary, *The Ghosts of Rwanda*, as vehicles that for me elicited the shame I am talking about. But, as Omer Bartov has pointed out to me, *Night and Fog* misrepresents in its own way and for historical reasons the events it claims to portray; it is a victim of what W. G. Sebald calls "half-consciousness or false consciousness" in its remembering the Nazi past and the atrocities of the death camps. Resnais and Cayrol engage in this "false consciousness" sometimes willfully, for political reasons, and sometimes unconsciously, as acts of repression. In other terms, films—like literature and other such vehicles—can themselves be shameful, reasons for shame regarding themselves as well as shame about the events they depict or express. Expression itself can be a reason for shame, as an action can be or a personal feature or one's ethnic background or racial characteristics. Not only can we be ashamed of the atrocities themselves, of having forgotten them, of having failed to remember the lessons of the past, and of living in nations and in a world that has now, years later, failed to intervene in behalf of the victims of subsequent genocides and atrocities; but also, we should be ashamed of the efforts in film and in the other arts that misrepresent and thereby deny, that serve the purposes of politics or artistic reputation (part of W. G. Sebald's point about postwar German literature), and that engage thereby in half-consciousness or false consciousness. And we should be ashamed too at accepting such efforts, endorsing them, failing to react to them and thereby furthering the failure of remembering and all it means to today's victims.[6]

W. G. Sebald pursues the theme of forgetting. His final work, *On the Natural History of Destruction*, concerns itself with the neglect of postwar German literature to remember and invest itself in the destructions of the war—with regard to the death camps and atrocities perpetrated by Germans, as he reflects in chapters on Jean Améry and Peter Weiss, and with regard to the horrors of the British bombing of Hamburg, Dresden, and other cities, as he explores in his Zurich lectures of 1997. In the latter, Sebald ponders the paucity of postwar literature about the horrors experienced by the victims of the British bombing in Hamburg especially. Such a dearth makes certain texts stand out as rare expressions of honesty. Commenting on the diary of Friedrich Reck, which is remarkable in this respect, Sebald says:

> Indeed, it seems that no German writer, with the sole exception of [Hans Erich] Nossack [in *The End: Hamburg 1943*], was ready or able to put any concrete facts down on paper about the progress and repercussions of this gigantic, long-term campaign of destruction. It was the same when the war was over. The quasi-natural reflex, engendered by feelings of shame and a wish to defy the victors, was to keep quiet and look the other way.
>
> (30)

Nossack, Sebald notes later, is like the messenger in a classical tragedy, who knows that such messengers are often killed for what they reveal (52)—which strikes me as an allusion to

Socrates in the *Apology* and hence to Plato's warning in the Cave in the *Republic*.[7] In the wake of atrocity, both the victims and the perpetrators may be too ashamed to remember what has occurred. Rare is the artist committed to keeping the memories alive. Given such avoidance, we ourselves should read with shame a literature that avoids the atrocities of its past, that chooses silence in place of the honesty of memory. Sebald's observations point to the way that shame can naturally lead to such silence, to hiding the secret, and how such silence can itself cultivate just the forgetfulness that then leads to our feelings of shame even now, to accepting the silence of others and being implicated in it ourselves.

I have called upon Cavell and Sebald to show us how placing shame in and around a particular work can be a complicated task. Let me follow their lead and in that spirit turn to the 1947 postwar Hollywood film *Crossfire*, which deals explicitly with the theme of antisemitism. This moody film noir, set in a dreary Washington hotel just after World War II, focuses on a platoon of soldiers, that is temporarily being housed in the hotel before being released and sent home. The dark and expressionist lighting and tone of the film underscore the soldiers's sojourn in limbo, between Europe and America, wartime comradeship and social alienation, and the uncertainties and worries about readjusting to a postwar American society. Several of them, drinking in a bar one night, meet a Jew, Samuels, and they proceed to join him in his room for more drinks. There is a fight, and Samuels is brutally killed. A young soldier, Mitchell, is the chief suspect; he is the film's noir hero, confused and uncertain of his future, wandering the streets during the night after leaving the room. In a bar he meets a sympathetic woman, whom he follows to her place; later his wife is called to Washington, and they reunite in the darkness of a movie theater. Mitchell is eventually cleared of the murder. The detective on the case is an Irish cop, Finlay, and Monty, the soldier who is exposed as the murderer, is portrayed as a homicidal, pathological racist. When he tries to flee the police, Finlay shoots him in the movie's final scene.

These are the bare bones of the plot. In addition to the murdered Jew, Samuels, Monty the pathological killer, played by Robert Ryan, the confused suspect, and the calm and probing detective, Finlay, played by Robert Young, the other main characters are the woman who consoles Mitchell, played by Gloria Graham, the sergeant of the platoon who assists the detective in the investigation, Keeley, played by Robert Mitchum, another young soldier who is persuaded to expose the murderer, and the suspect's wife who is called to Washington when her husband is under suspicion and is being pursued. Commentators regularly describe *Crossfire* as a "noir problem film" that synthesizes the plot, characters, and tone of the film noir crime genre with the social problem of antisemitism. But that is to simplify things.

Crossfire is a murder mystery. It begins with a murder, portrayed in a dark and expressionistic manner, and the flight of the murderer, and it proceeds with its investigation and a series of flashbacks that fill in the events leading up to the crime. As Mitchell's innocence and Monty's guilt become clear, the burden of the film's narrative shifts to Finlay's strategy for exposing Monty through a ruse. But if the murder mystery plot leads us to train our attention on Finlay's calm and probing rationality and Monty's ruthless insanity, the film's psychological portrayals focus in another direction. They dramatize the plight of the real hero of the film—its dark, brooding presence characteristic of the limbo in which these soldiers find themselves, the limbo of uncertainty and despair, the young Mitchell, wandering the night, "torn" between the consolations of the woman of the night and the domestic security of his wife, the victim of Monty's devious efforts to frame him, and symbolic of the existential alienation of postwar American literature and film, as viewed through the lens of French art and philosophy. If Finlay is the "seeker hero" of the film, then Mitchell is its "victim hero," lost, confused and helpless. Still, in this intertwining of murder mystery narrative and film noir psychological focus, the film finds a special role for its most explicit "social" theme—antisemitism. For Monty's motive for killing Samuels is precisely his pathological hatred of Jews, as Finlay makes explicitly clear in the film's most didactic moment. It is also the moment when shame enters into the film and into the audience's reaction to it.

Once it has become clear to Finlay and to Keeley that Mitchell is innocent and that Monty is the killer, Finlay devises a scheme to expose Monty. But he needs the help of a young soldier in the platoon, whom Monty has persecuted and humiliated but who is afraid of Monty. Finlay has the soldier come to his office, and he delivers a long speech about antisemitism, persecution and bigotry, seeking to persuade the soldier to lure Monty into exposing himself. At first the boy is afraid and wants no part in the scheme, but Finlay tells him a story about Finlay's own grandfather, who was beaten and killed by bigots who hated the Irish immigrants, and reminds the boy of the way Monty had humiliated him because of his rural Tennessee background. The boy looks down, turns away, seeks to avoid Finlay's stare—clearly, Finlay has made him ashamed enough to reconsider. The boy even suggests that Jews might deserve the treatment they receive, that is, he seeks to hide his shame behind blaming the victim. But in the end he gives in; the shame is too much, and he seeks to crawl out from under his shame by complying with Finlay's request, supported by Keeley and indeed by the colonel who is called in to support it.

But Finlay's long monologue, his chiding pedagogy about prejudice and bigotry, is not simply meant for the boy; it is meant for the film's audience as well. In an America seeking to unite itself and heal its wounds after the war, the message about bigotry is really a message about overcoming the separations between economic classes, between men and women, between black and white, and more. Bigotry, prejudice, and specifically antisemitism are codes for all that threatens to fragment America at a time when a postwar revival, economic and social, requires unity. In the Cold War, that ideology of unity will express itself in the clash with a single enemy externally in behalf of a commitment to the unity of democratic equality. But it will also require a commitment to a psychology of unity, opposition to prejudice and bigotry and intolerance of all kinds. The film, however, underscores how difficult it will be to generate that commitment; its message may be one of affirmation, but its tone is one of fatigue and disorientation. Instead of fanfare, therefore, it turns to shame. Finlay's speech to the film's audience wants those who have yet to commit themselves to these practices, like the young soldier from Tennessee, to feel ashamed of themselves, to feel the burden of self-reproach and the need to change who they are and how they treat others in an America that is as concerned with the threats of internal conflict as it is of external ones. There is no flag-waving in the wake of victory; rather there is a call for self-transformation through emotional decline.

In *Crossfire*, then, there is shame in the film, and there ought to be a reaction of shame by the audience itself. But there is more. *Crossfire* was directed by Edward Dmytryk, who was assigned to the film in 1947 by the new head of production at RKO Studios, Dore Schary, and had recently directed two successful noir thrillers, *Murder, My Sweet* and *Cornered*. RKO had on hand a screenplay by John Paxton called *Cradle of Fear*, based on a novel *The Brick Foxhole* by Richard Brooks, about the murder of a homosexual by a bigoted soldier. Schary asked Paxton, Dmytryk, and Adrian Scott, who had worked together on *Murder, My Sweet* to revise the screenplay, replacing anti-gay bigotry with antisemitism, which in the wake of World War II had become an acceptable subject for Hollywood films. Even though other RKO executives advised against the project, Schary pushed ahead, in the hopes of beating into the theaters a Fox production on the theme of antisemitism, *Gentlemen's Agreement*, then in production. In fact, Dmytryk succeeded, rushing the project to completion on a B-picture budget and schedule; it took twenty days to shoot on a budget of $250,000. The film grossed $1.27 million and was RKO's hit of the year; it was nominated for five Academy Awards and received a Grand Prize at Cannes. As we watch the film today, however, there are features of history that disturb. One is the fact that the film does not explore antisemitism as much as *use* it as a pretext for preaching against all kinds of prejudice and bigotry, and it does so by directly avoiding an issue of special social and political significance in today's America, the issue of the status of homosexuality.[8] A second is that the portrayal of antisemitism in the film encourages the thought, addressed by Elliot Cohen who was then editor of the new magazine *Commentary*, when he was informed of Schary's plans regarding the film, that antisemitism should be understood not as an attitude of normal people and hence as a serious social problem but rather as something eccentric, a pathological condition of the insane. A third concerns Dmytryk. He was summoned before the HUAC in 1948, as one of a famous group of ten unfriendly witnesses, probably because he directed *Crossfire*. When he refused to testify, Dmytryk was jailed and then released, six months later, recanted, and named names. These features of *Crossfire* send no uniform message, to be sure, but they do unsettle our viewing of the film today. If its original audience might have felt some sense of shame about a lingering bigotry present in postwar America, today's audience must feel a more complex set of emotions, with a renewed sense of shame, ramified perhaps by our knowledge about the film's avoidance of the issue of gays and lesbians and about its wholly inadequate portrayal of antisemitism. What this means is that perhaps today we would be more ashamed about the film than we would be shamed by it.

SHAME AND HOLOCAUST FILM

In chapter 2 I mentioned that recent accounts of shame are much indebted to Helen Lewis's concept of "bypassed" or unacknowledged shame and by her notion of the shame-rage spiral. The one supports the view that shame is a pervasive master-emotion, at the root of so much human psychology and conduct; the other has helped theorists and therapists alike to understand the extent and character of much of the violence and anger expressed in Western societies today. Such notions are especially helpful when one turns to portrayals of Holocaust survivors in a film such as *The Pawnbroker* and to a novel such as Aryeh Lev Stollman's *The Far Euphrates*. In each of these works, victims of the Holocaust are also the victims of a deep, traumatic shame that throbs at the core of their being, is concealed and refuses to be ignored or denied, threatens to erupt, and expresses itself in violence or depression or both.

The Pawnbroker, which appeared in 1965, depicts two days in the life of a Holocaust survivor, Sol Nazerman. It was directed by Sidney Lumet, who at the time had already been the director of three successful films, Twelve Angry Men (1957), A View from the Bridge (1962), and Long Day's Journey into Night (1963). The film, which takes place primarily in New York, much of it in Nazerman's Harlem pawn shop, is marked by stark realism combined with an almost expressionist use of darkness and shadow and a striking jazz score by Quincy Jones. Its cinematic and musical tone is one of shock and dissonance. Lumet's most innovative cinematic technique, which he adapted from its use by Alain Resnais in Hiroshima, Mon Amour (1959), is the use of flash cuts to express the disruptive way in which Nazerman's memories of the events of the past—the Nazis' initial taking his family into custody, their train ride to the death camps, and experiences of his imprisonment—fracture his mental life. Nazerman's memories are provoked by the date the film begins, the memorial of his wife's death, and in the day or two that follows, which the film depicts, they show us a man tormented by intense pain and drowning in overwhelming rage. Nazerman's anger is indiscriminate; it is aimed at everyone—the customers who seek his help in the pawn shop, his female friend, his landlord, the benevolent social worker who extends herself to help him, and his young, eager assistant, Jesus Ortiz, who in the end sacrifices his life for Nazerman.

As we see from the flash cuts of Nazerman's memories, moreover, the pain and the rage are deeply rooted, in hatred perhaps—of the Nazis and of the world itself—but also, profoundly, in a deep sense of shame.[9] His is a shame doubly forced upon him. On the one hand, it is shame about his young son's death in the packed railroad car on the journey to the death camp; on the other, it is shame over the sexual exploitation of his wife by the Nazi guards in the camp. In the film, we are introduced early to Nazerman's callousness, an insensitivity that is relentless and bitter; as we follow him through the day, moreover, that callousness escalates into verbal abuse and rage. At the same time, in the intrusive, brittle memories of his past, we watch a crescendo of pain that reaches its peak in two incidents. The first concerns his son. Wandering New York at night, having sought consolation at the apartment of the social worker who had visited his shop but left unsatisfied, Sol finds himself on the subway. The faces of other passengers remind him of those in the jammed railroad car on the way to the concentration camp. His young son, barely more than an infant, is asleep on his shoulder, and as the boy slips from his arms and is trampled, he recalls the agony of his wife's face and his own as he cries out, helpless to save the boy. Back in the subway car, Nazerman covers his face with his hands, hiding from others and from himself, from his memories and his sense of shame about the boy's death and his own helplessness.

The second memory is of his wife. We have seen her at the picnic when the family was taken by the Nazis and again in the railcar when their son is trampled to death. Now, Nazerman is in his pawn shop; he is visited by Jesus' girlfriend, who pleads with Nazerman for a better price for an item to be pawned and exposes herself to him. Her naked body triggers his memory, of seeing his wife in the camp, of her having been used sexually by a Nazi officer, devastated and utterly shamed by her nakedness and by the abuse to her very self. Once again, Nazerman's memory brings with it pain and rage, the pain of helplessness at the sight of the abuse of his wife, the pain of a shame rooted in his own sense of having been degraded along with her degradation.

The Pawnbroker never brings redemption from Nazerman's suffering and his shame. Lumet never allows Nazerman to be more than an angry, unappealing person, but as the flash cuts introduce to us more and more of his past and show how relentless and painful his memories are, we understand better why Nazerman is the man that he is. His is a pain and a rage born of shame, and by the film's end, when Jesus sacrifices his life to save Nazerman's and Nazerman impales his hand in an attempt to feel something for Jesus and about his sacrifice, we realize how thick and impenetrable are the layers of anger and hatred that he has created in order to hide that shame from himself rather than have to live with it.[10] As Nazerman leaves the shop and walks away from us, down the street, the camera pans to a wide view of the scene; there is no resolution to Nazerman's suffering and the shame that is its deepest source. It has been exposed but not redeemed. The sacrifice has been made but whether it has been effective is not resolved.

Rod Steiger's silent shriek surely elicits in us who watch the film and his impalement an instant of pained empathy. We feel his pain. In one way, *The Pawnbroker* is about surviving the Nazi concentration and death camps and living with one's memories, and hence it is about our living with those memories as conveyed to us in memoirs, diaries, stories, films, and more. And thus, if it is about Sol Nazerman's shame, it is also about ours, or the shame that we need to retrieve and to acknowledge, in order to come to grips with it, to "own it," as Michael Lewis has put it.[11] But the film can be interpreted within a different context. We should not forget that Nazerman's pawn shop is in Harlem, that his customers are blacks in America as is his landlord and Jesus' friends who burglarize the shop and ultimately kill Jesus. In 1965 the Civil Rights Movement in America had already shifted into a more nationalist stage; its liberal spokespersons shared the podium with figures such as Stokely Carmichael, James Forman, and Malcolm X. And the tensions between Jews and Blacks in America, which would explode years later in Ocean Hill/Brownsville and elsewhere, were becoming increasingly visible. Lumet's film juxtaposed the memories and the shame of the Nazi persecution of Jews and their victimization with the memories and the shame of the slavery and oppression of Blacks in America and their victimization. Watching the film in 1965, it would have been hard not to see the parallel and to leave the theater with a sense of shame about one's role, in America, as a bystander or a beneficiary or perhaps even an agent of exploitation and oppression. Could it have been in Lumet's mind to force upon that audience such a comparison and to dramatize the irony that among those who might very well feel the most shame about the exploitation of Blacks in America are the very descendants of those who themselves have lived with the most horrific persecution known to humankind?

Watching *The Pawnbroker* today, at a time when the shame and rage of the oppressed has reached a fever pitch throughout the world, should be a chastening experience, and emotionally a complex one. Something similar can be said about watching films that portray the suffering and degradation of women in cultures that complain themselves about the exploitation and domination of the West—films such as *Two Women*, *The Circle*, *Fire*, and *Osama*.[12] In such cases, of course, the viewer is made to feel a shame that may not have existed before, whereas I have read *The Pawnbroker* as serving to deepen a shame that is already felt, about forgetting what should never be forgotten and then extending it to feeling shame about other venues of oppression and injustice which one has ignored. But forgetting is one thing, camouflaging one's memories or distorting them is another, and there are films that might be thought to elicit shame for this reason too, for enticing us to misremember and hence to avoid shame in favor of indifference or detachment.

Here any number of films about the Holocaust come to mind—from the television series *Holocaust* to *Schindler's List* and the comedy *Life Is Beautiful*. If we realize that a film or novel, say, misrepresents or distorts the Holocaust, how should we react emotionally? How would the shame of forgetting the warnings of past atrocities be complicated by the shame of realizing that an imaginative work has mitigated the horrors or exploited them or defamed their victims, and perhaps the shame of having been seduced by that work? As one might expect, there is much room for debate. A film that may be successful and praiseworthy to one viewer, may be a failure and abominable to another. This is a platitude, of course, but when applied to films like the ones I just mentioned, it results in important differences. Take *Schindler's List* for example. Many commentators find fault with Spielberg's use of a narrative with a righteous gentile, indeed a reformed Nazi, as it were, as the hero, with his obvious allusions to the style of film noir, his use of color and black and white, the melodramatic contrast of pathological Nazis and righteous Jewish victims, and the exploitative use of female nakedness in the shower scene. But others have argued that the film is consciously postmodern in its use of motifs and techniques from various cinematic genres and alluding in various ways to previous Holocaust films, that it teaches us something important about post-Holocaust cinema while exploring the varieties of humanity and inhumanity with which we all have to cope.[13] Similarly, responses to Benigni's *Life Is Beautiful* have ranged from the severely critical to the wildly positive. Some are offended by the glib humor of the scene in which Benigni mistranslates the German instructions to the inmates in his barracks, as a way of convincing his son about the pretense of the game, while others treat the game and all its features as a brilliant device for exploring the way that fantasy and humor can help us to face the most tragic situations. Should we react with a sense of shame to the shower scene in *Schindler's List* and the scene in the barracks in *Life Is Beautiful* or should we admire them and feel moved or elevated? I am not here interested in defending an interpretation of films such as these. My point is a different one. If one comes to see a film or a play, or a novel or story, as a distortion or simplification or a misleading fabrication, then we might very well feel angry. But we ought also to feel ashamed for its very existence as the misrepresentation that it is, and even more we should feel ashamed of ourselves if indeed we have initially been seduced into accepting it and allowing it to bear the burden of veracity for us. In such cases, there are films which are obviously filled with errors of fact and judgment, others that are more controversial, and others that have been taken to be successful and serious but have been occasionally challenged nonetheless. It may be that the more one understands about the way a film came into being, about the intentions of its producer or screenwriter or director, and about the historical context of its production, the more one will come to doubt its sincerity and honesty, and hence the more one might feel ashamed for it and of oneself for having failed to understand its limitations. Or, in other cases, greater understanding of context and such might very well turn an initial sense of shame and self-reproach into a positive assessment, both of the film and of ourselves as viewers of it. Viewing many of the Hollywood comedies of the 1930s and 1940s, for example, one might now feel ashamed about the treatment of women and minorities, but that shame might at least be reduced in intensity, if not largely avoided, as a result of understanding the films differently, as attempts by creative directors to articulate themes that were explicitly forbidden by the code at the time and that could only be indirectly addressed within the economic constraints of the classic Hollywood film industry as it was then conducted.[14] Shame is no constant. When it persists, it changes—becoming deeper or less serious, more complex in its rationale and in its focus.

TRAUMATIC SHAME AND THE LITERARY IMAGINATION

Let me conclude this discussion with one last example, this time from post-Holocaust literature. Aryeh Lev Stollman's *The Far Euphrates* is a novel about a boy, Alexander, growing to manhood, in Windsor, Ontario, among Holocaust survivors—his parents (his father is the rabbi of their synagogue) and their friends, their Cantor, his wife Berenice and sister Hannalore. It is about his mother's worries about him—"something she dared not speak, some looming tragedy for us both," he says[15]—about the development of his own sense of sexuality, of his life as a writer, and about the ways in which the Holocaust, through the memories of those around him, pervades this growth and shapes it. And the novel is also about a secret, one that is hidden in unspoken memories, and that we learn—and his mother learns—only late in the narrative, long after Alexander, and that is a secret about shame, pain, fear, and acknowledgment for his family, their friends, and for him.[16]

For our purposes, the figure who most of all harbors deep

fears and traumatic shame is Alexander's mother Sarah. When she learns, at the unveiling of Hannalore's tombstone, that she, Hannalore, and the Cantor had been twins experimented upon by the Nazis and that Hannalore had lived her life as a woman, hiding the secret of her sexuality and the mutilation that had transformed her, Sarah also discovers that Berenice had revealed the secret to Alexander years before. And Sarah hides her shame about Alexander's homosexuality behind anger and blame. Her attempt to have another child, to replace Alexander, fails. Imitating his own seclusion, when he hides in his room for a year as his own sexuality blossoms, she isolates herself, waiting for the birth that never comes. And all along, she turns away from Berenice for having revealed the secret about Hannalore to Alexander, whose own sexual transformation, she believes, is a subconscious duplication of Hannalore's mutilation at the hands of the Nazi doctors. Sarah's shame, her sense of utter failure and lack of worth, is grounded in the memories of pain and humiliation and in the fear and anger that live within her. What she fears is bringing something to life; she fears what might happen to that life, for she has experienced what an assault on it can be. Hence, she fears that something might be wrong with Alexander, and, in her own eyes, her fears are realized. What she fears is degradation, and she takes his sexual identity to be such a degradation. Of it she is deeply and profoundly ashamed; she sees it as the legacy of Nazi atrocity, as a duplication in her own son of the degradation to which Hannalore had been subjected. Alexander's homosexuality, to Sarah, is an unspeakable horror, an indirect but certain outcome of the evils of Nazism and the horrors of the camps.

Stollman's novel, however, wants us to appreciate Alexander's sexuality and his emergence as a writer both together as features of his growth. Sarah's shame and her fears are overcome in Alexander. His writing enables him to do what she cannot, to remember the past and live in the present together, without seeing the former as the nemesis of the latter. Unlike her, he copes with any shame he might have once had about his homosexuality, and turns it into a work of the imagination in which the secret of the Nazi humiliation is acknowledged and turned into new life, consumed and transformed like food.

Remembering the suffering of the victims of the Nazi atrocities, we too might be ashamed by their degradation. We might try to hide our faces and refuse to confront what took place. But *The Far Euphrates* does not allow us such evasion, nor does it allow us to avoid confronting the complexity of human sexuality. It recommends that the creative imagination can help us to overcome these evasions and to acknowledge our sense of shame. And it recommends too that the capacity of language to help us to cope with our memories, the reality of our lives, and those around us is, at its deepest level, a religious capacity. This is something that permeates the novel and Stollman's sensibility as an author, one that resists allowing piety and language to drift apart from one another.

But piety is one thing, ethical recovery another, and for the latter one must turn elsewhere. Shame, especially traumatic shame, can drive us to blame others, to despair of ourselves, or to strike out violently, but the shame I am recommending as a reaction to the horrors of Auschwitz, Bosnia, Cambodia, Rwanda, and Darfur is of a different sort. If this kind of collective shame can be cultivated as a stage in our moral improvement, it can serve that process only if it leads to a response that leaves it behind.

Beyond Shame

Emotional Reaction and Moral Response

Four

Shame has consequences. In Kazuo Ishiguro's novel *An Artist of the Floating World* the main character Masuji Ono recalls a conversation with Miyake, who was to be engaged to Ono's daughter but whose family withdrew from the negotiations. During the conversation Miyake comments on the death of the president of his company, who committed suicide out of shame for his support of the government during World War II (55–56). Miyake takes the president's action to have been a fine thing to have done, a relief to those in the company, an act of apology, of responsibility, a noble gesture. But to Masuji Ono the man's suicide was extreme and a waste. Psychologists tell us that suicide can indeed be a response to extreme shame and as such an act of unconditional hiding, indeed of permanent concealment.[1] Responses to shame can be productive or destructive. One can face up to one's shame and "own it" or capitulate to it—in anger, depression, violence, or even self-annihilation. If we overcome denial, however, and find a way to acknowledge our shame, what might be a noble or responsible way of acting on it?

SHAME AS MORAL MOTIVATION

If we want to understand how shame can be a moral emotion and a motivation to accomplish something beneficial for ourselves and others, we need to look at what psychologists and other social scientists tell us are typical responses to shame. Furthermore, we need to ask ourselves how the kind of shame I have been discussing, an emotional reaction introduced in order to bring us to admit our failures and respond to them, can lead us to such beneficial results. Indeed, in response to the shame we ought to feel in the face of the cumulative suffering and atrocities that have punctuated these last several decades, what ought we to do? How can this shame contribute to our taking responsibility and acting on it?

As we have already said, one might have very grave doubts about the utility of shame, for shame regularly leads to horrific responses to rid ourselves of it or to compensate for it. This is true both when the shame is private and personal and when it is an emotion that we share with others, our family, our compatriots, or all of humankind. When it comes to collective shame, perhaps the most noteworthy case is that of Germany after Versailles and the shame of defeat in World War I. Richard J. Evans, in *The Third Reich in Power, 1933–1939*, puts it this way:

> However concerned they were at the threat of a general war, there was no mistaking the pride and satisfaction of the great majority of Germans . . . at Hitler's achievement in throwing off the universally hated yoke of Versailles. Resignation from the League of Nations, the plebiscite in the Saar, the remilitarization of the Rhineland, the annexation of Austria, the incorporation of the Sudetenland, the regaining of Memel, the takeover of Danzig—all of this seemed to Germans to be wiping out the shame of the 1919 Peace Settlement . . .
>
> (711)

Evans argues again and again how shame motivated support for Hitler and Nazism and was used by them to generate propaganda and sympathy for their aims. It is a terrifying example of the lengths to which people will go in order to recover a sense of dignity and self-worth. From a psychological perspective, Michael Lewis, in *Shame*, proposes that Hitler cultivated the German sense of shame into blame of traitors, Communists, and Jews and turned that shame into aggression against those who were responsible in his eyes (230). Lewis also proposes that the first Iraq war, Desert Storm, is the result of shame for Viet Nam, and we might suggest too that the current Iraq war is the result of shame over the loss of the first (230). In short, shame can occur not only at a personal level but also at a national one, and it can follow a path of blame and violence rather than that of honest self-assessment and responsible recovery.

The sociologist Thomas J. Scheff, in "Shame and the Social Bond: A Sociological Perspective," argues that there is a social dimension to shame, beyond its psychoanalytic and psychological character.[2] In reflecting upon the Nazi use of the shame of Versailles, Scheff calls attention to an argument that is made in Norbert Elias' book, *The Germans*: in it Elias argues that Germans, individually and as a nation, have been unable to deal with humiliation except by fighting—suggesting that the escalation of Nazi atrocities was, on a national scale, an example of the shame-anger/rage spiral (96). Scheff concludes that shame refers to a family of emotions—including embarrassment, humiliation and feelings of shyness—that involve feelings of inadequacy or failure (96). But while a psychological definition, he says, focuses on failure to satisfy an ideal, his sociological definition characterizes shame as the feeling of a threat to the social bond (97). That is, shame involves turning away from the face of another, lowering one's eyes, not being able to confront the other who has judged us to be inadequate or whom we believe thinks of us as flawed. In this way, then, shame marks social fragmentation, one person turning away from another. Hence for Scheff the sense of shame is constant, since the anticipation of such threats is always present to one degree or another. This is very different, he says, from the vernacular use, according to which shame is a crisis emotion closely connected with disgrace (97). For Scheff, then, the response of Germans during the Weimar years, to blame others and to strike out in anger and ultimately in rage at those thought to be responsible—Communists, Jews, and others, was an attempt to reconstitute the internal social bond, the ability of Germans to live with one another, through external domination.[3] It was an effort to live face to face with other Germans by blaming Jews and others for the failure of which they were ashamed.

Shame that turns people to xenophobia and blame is hardly worthy. And if we turn from national shame after a specific war to shame in the face of war itself, the results are no more encouraging. War is preeminent among the objects of shame that grip us in the modern world and especially in the twentieth century and today. There are many films, for example, that dramatize the pointlessness of war and that seek to portray its horrors. Such films frequently aim at cultivating opposition to war as politically useless and a moral evil.[4] But there are films themselves to which shame is also an appropriate reaction, along with a sense of horror and despair. In this respect it is worth comparing Terrence Malick's treatment of war in *The Thin Red Line* with Ingmar Bergman's attempt to explore the horror of war and its degradation, the disintegration of us in war, in *Shame*, his film of 1970. One of the themes of *Shame* is the indistinguishability of the enemies in war and the horrific conduct of both, the uniform death and degradation.[5] In Malick's film, on the other hand, the camera looks behind or beyond the grand themes of war, its political and moral dimensions, to the minutiae of experience in the war. Yet, such an attentiveness to the prosaic and the mundane does run a risk. One cannot help but wonder if there is not in Malick a kind of poeticizing and aestheticizing of war.[6] How is this related to the shame (and guilt) we should feel about war in our world?

A central theme of Bergman's *Shame* is to explore a response to shame that leads irrevocably to vengeance, killing, and atrocity. The film's main character Jan, played by Max von Sydow, sinks into shame over his willingness to sacrifice everything for safety—even allowing his wife Eva, Liv Ullmann, to be seduced by the government official Jacobi. When given the opportunity to betray Jacobi to a group of partisans by withholding money that Jacobi had given to Eva, he does so and then, when told by them to shoot Jacobi, he capitulates and, for his own safety and out of shame and vengeance, he kills him. From then on, Jan's decline into savagery and atrocity is precipitous. His shame is evident, and his response horrific. Bergman's film may not focus on Jan's response to shame in particular but rather on the way shame is the hinge between impotence and savagery, but the destructive consequences of shame are palpable. In this case, then, shame does not provoke an humane response but rather quite the opposite—revenge, hatred, selfishness, and brutality. What Bergmann shows is how war—and life itself—leads directly from threats to one's safety to acts that elicit shame to evasion and savagery and rage. It is a powerful depiction of the kind of spiral of shame, anger, and rage that psychologists have explored; and that is one of the reasons one might doubt that a genuinely moral response to shame is possible at all.

The prospects appear no better if we turn from collective or personal reactions to large-scale events to individual shame. The connection between shame and responses such as extreme narcissism, depression, the blaming of others, violence, and rage should make us wonder if there is anything positive about shame at all and indeed if a positive response to it is at all likely.[7] In their book, *Shame and Guilt*, Jean Tangney and Ronda Dearing recommend guilt over shame as a useful emotion. They treat shame and guilt as emotions of self-blame (*Shame and Guilt*, 53–54). But, while shame tends to be an internal, stable, and global attribution (53), guilt is internal but unstable and specific. Hence, guilt is more easily dislodged, and doing so, given its precise focus, is more likely. They propose that overall guilt is more adaptive than shame, since it is targeted at behavior which can be rectified more easily than changes in the self and personality (56). Such an analysis, then, is a problem for any attempt to acknowledge a sense of shame that is collective regarding the type of world we live in and that is also adaptive. To use their expression, the question is whether there is anything beyond the "dark side of shame" (Tangney and Dearing, 125).[8] Psychologists Sylvan Tomkins and later Donald Nathanson argue that there is—that shame helps to regulate experiences of excessive interest and excitement (Tangney and Dearing, 126). But although some psychologists have claimed that shame helps people avoid wrongdoing and failure, Tangney and Dearing do not find empirical support for this moral role (126 and chapter 8).

MOTIVATED TO DO WHAT?

Amidst their overall negative appraisal, however, Tangney and Dearing do make one encouraging observation, as I already indicated:

> The acute pin of shame may in some cases motivate productive soul-searching and revisions of one's priorities and values. The challenge is to engage in such introspection and self-repair without becoming sidetracked by defensive reactions . . . Such a positive function of shame might ensue from private, self-generated experiences of shame as opposed to public, other-generated shame episodes. Perhaps non-shame-prone, high-ego-strength individuals with a solid sense of self may occasionally use shame constructively in the privacy of their own thoughts.
>
> (126)

This is an important insight that may help us to explain how shame can be a vehicle for responding morally to genocides, massacres, and violence in our world and for taking such responsibilities seriously. If shame is a shock or jolt to our sensibility, it may be that it can lead to "productive soul-searching" and "self-repair."[9]

As I mentioned in chapter 2, the term "shame" covers a variety of emotional experiences, elicited in a wide range of circumstances. The morally relevant emotion which I have tried to identify is marked by several features. It is targeted at moral failures—here the failure to do what is necessary to alter a culture of genocide and atrocity and when necessary to intercede to prevent massacres from occurring or continuing. At the same time, this shame, which is not spontaneous but rather is acknowledged and perhaps self-introduced, does not have two problematic features of other forms of shame: it is not completely isolating, and it is not self-disabling. That is, unlike that shame which makes us want to hide and remove ourselves from the company of others, this shame is a jointly held emotion that brings us together with *some* others with the encouragement that we can do what is necessary to allow us to face those in need.[10] Moreover, unlike shame that leads to depression and immobilizes us, this shame can motivate us to act, and with the proper commitment, that action would be aimed at acting in behalf of those in need. To be sure, there are risks in cultivating an emotional reaction as a stage in the process of moral education, but the shame I have tried to describe and endorse is a plausible candidate for such a project. Indeed, without an emotional investment, even if rational assessment calls attention to a need, there is little reason to think that moral development will occur.[11]

Suppose, then, that we do elicit shame in ourselves for the kind of world we live in, a world of genocide and mass destruction of life. Where does such shame take us? What does it motivate us to do? In order to provide some guidance for answering this question, let me begin with a point that I have cited more than once, that many psychologists and sociologists take shame to be a pervasive feature of our lives. What these social scientists mean by this is that phenomena such as the extent and nature of violence that occurs in society can be taken as evidence of coping with shame and a sense of self-denigration. One thinker who would agree, in his own special way, with this claim about the pervasiveness of shame is the French philosopher Emmanuel Levinas. Unlike psychologists and sociologists, however, his reasons for thinking this are not empirical, at least not in the same way, but rather philosophical.

For Levinas, each of us, as a person in society with others, is responsible—in an unbounded way—to and for each and every other person. Levinas has much to say about why this is so and what it means. Let me here simply assume that it is so and follow Levinas' thinking a step beyond that assumption. Such a situation, he says, elicits shame in two ways. First, each of us confronts every other person with shame at *always already* being called into question by that other person. We always face the other person as already obligated, as called upon to help or assist him, to give the bread from our own mouths to feed him. Second, if our responsibility to others is unlimited and infinite, then we will always fail to satisfy it. No matter how much we give, it is never enough; no matter whom we help, there is always someone else who needs our help. No matter how we choose to help, there are always other needs still to be met. If shame is the self-reflective recognition of our failure before others and before ourselves, then for Levinas shame is a permanent feature of our social and moral lives. It is the expression of that responsibility and the fact of having always and necessarily failed to accomplish it fully. For this reason, when acknowledged, shame should always be a motivation to attend to our responsibility to and for other persons in some relevant, plausible, and workable way.

But determining the latter will be a complicated business, involving calculation and examination of a very detailed kind, and compromise. I think that the kinds of issues discussed by Garrett Cullity in *The Moral Demands of Affluence* are germane in this regard, for the burden of his argument is to articulate a workable principle of beneficence. It is one thing to acknowledge the obligation to beneficence (to use Cullity's terminology); it is another to determine how exactly to respond in our world, with limited resources and complex restrictions of a personal and social nature, to that obligation—what reasons there might be to qualify, override, or modify it. Shame can lead to a host of possible responses; determining which is most salient and telling is a concrete matter not to be avoided or neglected.

Levinas' fundamental insight, that each of us is infinitely responsible to each and every other person, is not likely to appeal to everyone as a true and accurate understanding of the ground of ethical conduct or as the basic feature of our social existence. But one does not have to be a Levinasian, of course, to see how shame can be a motivation to care for others. One might think, alternatively, that morality is a matter of doing what would increase the total amount of goodness in the world and what would reduce suffering and pain and that we all have a moral obligation to do just that in every situation in which we find ourselves, as long as it does not require our doing anything that is morally culpable. A view like this has been advocated by Peter Singer and other consequentialists, and here too one can see how holding it might contribute to a sense of shame about failing to do all that is required of us.[12] Indeed, if we believe that morality is always somehow associated with a concern for the well-being of others, diminishing their suffering and contributing to their flourishing, and if the demands of morality always require our sacrificing ourselves to a degree that we rarely if ever actually meet, then shame would be a very common feature of our moral lives. Moreover, the shame we feel, as always being morally inadequate, would be a motivation for us. It would be a kind of shock to our complacency, a jolt to our sensibility that would point toward our elevating our sense of obligation and our commitment to meeting those obligations. It is in this spirit that I introduce Levinas, who explicitly speaks of shame as being a pervasive feature of our social and moral lives.

For Levinas, then, taking responsibility and acting on it and responding to one's sense of shame at failing to do so are features of all social existence. Negotiating our lives with others by acting in behalf of justice and generosity is none other than taking our shame to heart and responding to it. Coming to grips with one's shame means appreciating the needs of others and reaching out to them in one of any number of ways. It is, that is, to become a more sensitive and caring person, to organize one's life and one's projects around such a sense of oneself, never forgetting first and foremost what others need, their pain and suffering, their vulnerability and dependence.[13]

It was not accidental, therefore, that I concluded chapter 1 with a reference to Levinas and to the desirability and the necessity—morally speaking—of responding to our shame by responding to others, of facing up to our failures by reaching out to assist those who are victims, to reduce suffering, to speak out and act in behalf of those oppressed, abandoned, and in need. Stanley Cavell, in *Senses of Walden*, says of despair and the loss of respect, that they are not "static conditions" but rather "goads to action" (70), and this is also true of shame. In normal cases, we respond to shame by seeking to rid ourselves of it, to eradicate the pain or disturbance we feel that comes along with our sense of failure. We want to correct the fault, to alter others' view of us, and to recover our own sense of our worth to ourselves. However, with regard to the kind of shame I have been discussing, a sense of collective shame for the genocidal atrocities and the violence that mark our world, when the shame is for us all and before us all, seeking to erase the pain and sense of failure is not something we can do on our own, and yet it is not something we can each fail to attempt. On the one hand, we cannot accomplish it alone. On the other, we cannot avoid acting, knowing our limitations.

But, in such a case, what should we do? What is it to remember the Holocaust and its victims? What is it not to abandon those suffering in Darfur, nor to forget the world's failure to intercede in Rwanda, nor to fail to learn the lessons of the Nazi genocide? If the needs are so very great and our shame so deep, what indeed can we do?[14] Here it is worth receiving guidance from the philosopher Emil Fackenheim, from the survivor Jean Améry, from poets and novelists like Paul Celan and Primo Levi, from Levinas, and others. Responding to shame is contextual and hermeneutical. In view of the shame elicited by the continued and escalating genocidal actions and the failure to intervene and to oppose with honesty and decisiveness which also has ramifications extending back to the shame for Auschwitz and for living afterwards, that context is focused on care for others no matter how distant, how isolated, where and by whom their persecution and assault is carried out. It is worth taking up Levinas' insight about the primary ethical claim of our social existence and what that means in our complex social and political and moral lives. Since the shame is universal, it is fitting that our sense of responsibility should be universal, even if its infinitude, in Levinas' terms, makes the demands extreme and unfulfillable. It marks our finitude but in no way cancels our obligations. As Fackenheim claims, in the last chapter of God's Presence in History, our lives do not cease to have such obligations even if they are unavoidably in conflict with each other. Shame, that is, may expose our failure to take up a responsibility or set of responsibilities that are great and even beyond any satisfaction but that still require our attention if we are to maintain a sense of integrity and self-worth, in short if we are to do what we can to overcome the shame which we now may have come to acknowledge.

At the end of the preface to the second edition of *To Mend the World*, published in 1989, Emil Fackenheim comments on a saying of Hegel's and the way that it ought to be reinterpreted for our own day:

> Hegel once said that the wounds of Spirit heal without leaving scars. He could no longer say this today. To speak of a healing has become inappropriate. Scars of the wounds of Spirit remain and will continue to remain. But a mending is possible, and therefore necessary.
>
> (*To Mend the World*, 2nd edn., xxv)

Fackenheim criticizes Hegel for an optimism that is undeserved and indeed impossible today, in a world that is marked by the Holocaust, Hiroshima, Cambodia, Bosnia, Kosovo, and Rwanda. Like Levinas, he believes that twentieth-century history has refuted not one theodicy nor many; indeed it has discredited the very use of theodicies to deal with suffering and inhumanity. Hence, complete healing is impossible; the historical and human scars cannot be removed without a trace. But mending is not impossible; indeed it is necessary—morally necessary. In the terms we have been using, coping with our shame requires repair— of oneself and of our world, a fragmentary repair to be sure but a repair nonetheless. It will be fragmentary because there are limits to our resources, to our abilities, and to our will, and because the needs are great and always increasing. And the repair will be fragmentary too because some historical ruptures are both always with us and simply beyond mending.

Furthermore, shame itself can fall into the wrong hands.

Psychologists warn us that shame leads to denial and compensation—to pathologies. It may be that such warnings come naturally to someone in a therapeutic situation, whose findings are tailored to diagnosing such pathologies and finding ways to cope with them. The warnings, however, are salient, and, as I have noted, they can help us to understand something about the prominence of violence, abuse, and depression in our society. But not only can shame lead to terrible outcomes in this way; it can also itself be misused.

In "Mobilizing Shame" Thomas Keenan calls attention to the expression the "mobilization of shame," which is used in human rights circles. The phrase is the title of a book by Robert Drinan, a Jesuit and a seasoned participant in this arena. Keenan cites, as the earliest reference to the phrase he could find, a statement by Judge B. V. A. Roling from 1979. Roling associates the expression with the influencing of public opinion for humanitarian purposes. But Keenan sees its darker side:

> The lockstep logic of if-then, in which knowledge generates action (reaction), seems to suggest a wishful fusion of an Enlightenment faith in the power of reason and knowledge with a realistic pessimism that retreats to the shame appropriate to the unenlightened. This pattern repeats itself as the concept develops.
>
> (437)

This "retreat to shame" can be employed as a device for self-reproach in order to motivate a generous response. Recall the scene in *Hotel Rwanda* where, after the French have left Kigali, Paul Rusesabagina encourages those remaining to call all their friends and contacts throughout the world in order to shame them into responding. Keenan says that this tactic of "mobilizing shame is the predominant practice of human rights organizations" (437), and he discusses the way that this strategy is often combined with the use of "disaster pornography," the exhibitionist tendency to exploit images of destruction and atrocity (438–39). Shame can be a response and it can generate compensating reactions, but it can also be exploited in unacceptable ways. Even as the shame itself can be acknowledged as expressing a genuine failure of benevolence and human concern, it can also be manipulated. A person ashamed can be vulnerable and easily influenced. Hence, we must realize that the shame for humankind and for our complicity in genocide and atrocity can be used for good or ill.

For such reasons, the call for shame and one's response to it must be solicited with care. But the challenge could be—indeed must be—worth the risk. Articulate arguments—in behalf of controlling greenhouse gases and in behalf of global justice, removing poverty, and solving the problem of world hunger—are vital.[15] Moreover, as I have claimed, the prominence of genocide and similar atrocities in our world certainly calls for a humanitarian response. But what is rational and reasonable does not always take a grip of us and move us to act. We must emotionally want to do what we are persuaded is the right thing to do, and what I am proposing is that shame can be cultivated as the emotional core of such motivation.

Philosophers have argued that who we are and what we owe to others are inextricably intertwined. Shame has a structure especially suited to respond to both of these dimensions of the moral life, the personal and the interpersonal. It is *about* some condition that is true of us, often about some action or omission that can be attributed to us; it is *of* ourselves, our character or identity as a whole; and it is *before* others, either real or imagined. Given such a structure, shame as an emotion is uniquely capable of calling attention to personal inadequacies and so doing by calling us to self-reflection and to a sensitivity to how others view us simultaneously. It is appropriate that any response to that shame, to its moral dimension, should seek to repair both ourselves and others as well as the bonds between us.

For all the difficulties that this task may pose, then, it is indeed a worthwhile one. As human beings we are capable of coming to understand to one degree or other what is right and good and how to attain them, and we are also capable of sensing emotionally that we have failed and that we need to do better. Precisely because it is unpleasant and disturbing, feeling shame is one way of setting out on this path.

Notes

INTRODUCTION

1 Or perhaps feeling guilt or anger or fear might be a more appropriate response. I say something later about why shame is especially
appropriate.

2 For discussion, see Samantha Power, "A Problem from Hell": America and
the Age of Genocide (New York: HarperCollins, 2002). Also, for systematic
discussion of the principle of non-intervention and national sovereignty and its history in the postwar period and after the fall of the
Soviet Union, see Nicholas J. Wheeler, Saving Strangers: Humanitarian Intervention in International Society (Oxford: Oxford University Press, 2000);
Deen K. Chatterjee and Don E. Schied (eds.), Ethics and Foreign Intervention
(Cambridge: Cambridge University Press, 2003).

ONE SHAME, THE HOLOCAUST, AND DARK TIMES

1 There are several discussions of Night and Fog that I have found helpful,
among them: William Rothman, Documentary Film Classics (Cambridge:
Cambridge University Press, 1997), pp. 39–68; Jay Cantor, "Death and
the Image," in his On Giving Birth to One's Own Mother: Essays on Art and Society
(New York: Alfred A. Knopf, 1991), pp. 143–77; Ilan Avisar, Screening
the Holocaust: Cinema's Images of the Unimaginable (Bloomington: Indiana
University Press, 1988), pp. 6–18; André Pierre Colombat, The Holocaust
in French Film (Metuchen, NJ: Scarecrow Press, 1993), pp. 121–66.

2 In his discussion of Night and Fog, Rothman says that the task Resnais sets
for the film is "to restore the reality" of the camps, as if they had been
destroyed by their liberation and evacuation and by time itself. He says
that "the film undertakes this task so that we may no longer 'pretend to
know nothing about' the 'endless, uninterrupted fear' that was—is—

the 'true dimension'" of those camps (Rothman, *Documentary Film Classics*, p. 45; see also pp. 48, 53, 60). By restoring the reality of the world of the past, the film also restores the reality of the present (pp. 48–49).

3 See, for example, Samantha Power, *"A Problem from Hell": America and the Age of Genocide* (New York: HarperCollins, 2002), p. 357; Alain Destexhe, *Rwanda and Genocide in the Twentieth Century* (New York: New York University Press, 1995), p. 32; Michael Barnett, *Eyewitness to a Genocide: The United Nations and Rwanda* (Ithaca, NY: Cornell University Press, 2002), pp. 1, 8, 21, 169–70; Gérard Prunier, *The Rwanda Crisis: History of a Genocide* (New York: Columbia University Press, 1997); Philip Gourevitch, *We wish to inform you that tomorrow we will be killed with our families* (New York: Farrar, Straus and Giroux, 1998), p. 170 ("Rwanda has presented the world with the most unambiguous case of genocide since Hitler's war against the Jews. . . . The West's post-Holocaust pledge that genocide would never again be tolerated proved to be hollow, and for all the fine sentiments inspired by the memory of Auschwitz, the problem remains that denouncing evil is a far cry from doing good.") and p. 316. Commenting on radio about the 1963 killings in Rwanda, Bertrand Russell said that it was the most horrible and systematic extermination of a people since the Nazi extermination of the Jews; see the article, "L'Extermination des Tutsi," *Le Monde* (4 February 1964). Russell's comment is frequently cited, for example by Linda Melvern, *Conspiracy to Murder: The Rwandan Genocide* (London: Verso, 2004), p. 9, and also in her book *A People Betrayed: The Role of the West in Rwanda's Genocide* (London: Zed Books, 2000), p. 17. See also Gourevitch, *We wish to inform you*, p. 65.

4 The numerous books on the Rwandan genocide discuss its history and the precise ways in which it was prepared for—the racial system of classification that became a pervasive feature of Rwandan life but that was mobilized and utilized for social and political purposes by the Belgian colonial administration, the system of identity cards, the preparation of lists of Tutsi and Hutu accomplices or supporters of democratization of the RPF, and so on—but particularly noteworthy accounts are provided by Prunier, *The Rwanda Crisis* and Melvern, *Conspiracy to Murder*. According to Melvern, the first time the word *genocide* was applied to what was occurring in Rwanda was on April 9, 1993, in response to the slaughter of 10,000 people, in two days, in Gikondo, many of whom

were seeking shelter in a Catholic church and were massacred by the militia, the *Interahamwe*, "slashing with their machetes and clubs, hacking arms, legs, genitals, and the faces of terrified people who tried to protect the children under the pews. . . . Not even babies were spared" (p. 182). Only two people seem to have survived the slaughter. For a further description, based on the report of Major Brent Beardsley, assistant to the UN front commander Roméo Dallaire, see Dallaire's *Shake Hands with the Devil: The Failure of Humanity in Rwanda* (Toronto: Random House, 2003), pp. 278–81. Beardsley and a team of observers came upon the Polish church shortly after the massacre. Dallaire's description of the "unbelievable horror," of mutilations, the disemboweling of a pregnant woman and the severing of her fetus, is grisly and shocking. Dallaire concludes his account as follows: "The massacre was not a spontaneous act. It was a well-executed operation involving the army, Gendarmerie, Interahamwe and civil service" (p. 281).

5 See, for example, Melvern, *A People Betrayed*, pp. 77–80; Barnett, *Eyewitness to a Genocide*, pp. 34–48; Melvern, *Conspiracy to Murder*, pp. 68–71. For a discussion of the crisis in Bosnia, see Melvern, *A People Betrayed*, p. 174 and, more comprehensively, Power, *"A Problem from Hell"*, chapter 9.

6 For excellent, detailed, and persuasive accounts, see the books cited above in notes 3 and 4, especially Dallaire's disturbing memoir, *Shake Hands with the Devil*. Dallaire, who is widely cited in all the books on the Rwandan genocide, was the Canadian Lieutenant General appointed as the field commander of the United Nations Assistance Mission for Rwanda (UNAMIR).

7 I am thinking particularly of the admissions made by those who were, in their own ways, major players in the international political activity that permitted the genocide to go on, among them Kofi Annan, Madeleine Albright, and even Bill Clinton.

8 In his important essay on the films *Night and Fog, Hotel Terminus*, and *Shoah*, Jay Cantor calls attention to the horror and the fear: if death were really present in the images and pictures, then "one would feel, as the narrator of Alain Resnais's documentary *Night and Fog* reminds us, 'endless, uninterrupted fear' " ("Death and the Image," p. 145). In fact, Cantor notes, Resnais accomplishes something remarkable: "He makes the horrible ordinary, so we might believe it; and then he makes the ordinary horrible, so that we might fear it" ("Death and the Image," p. 148). In

the film, the ordinary is represented by train tracks, fields, fences, old buildings—in short, the remains of the past that today appear benign and almost lyrical. By exposing what lies "beneath" them, so to speak, Resnais makes them "terrifying," "horrifying." Memory leads to fear. My attention is not on this fear or terror but rather on the shame we feel when we realize that we have forgotten, repressed the memory, even when what we are looking at tells us that what we have forgotten is that the past is, in fact, present today, perhaps far from view, like Darfur, but present nonetheless.

9 About one-third into the film, there is an interview with a Rwandan woman in her early twenties, I would say. With a gentle face and eyes, she recalls a massacre at a church in Nyarbuye. Later in the film, we hear about a visit to that church by the British journalist Fergal Keane, who covered Rwanda for the *Sunday Times* and wrote a book about the genocide, *Season of Blood*. We see his visit, the remains of slaughtered victims piled outside the church and in the church, scattered under and around pews. He then mentions stopping at the local mayor's office, where he sees a mother and two children, survivors, one of the children, a young girl, emaciated, her hand black, fingers chopped off, and with a wound on the back of her head. We realize that this skeletal, suffering child, then thirteen years old, had survived and become the young woman we met earlier, Valentina Iribagiza. It is a moving moment. In a *Times* article, Keane writes:

> I left Rwanda shortly afterwards vowing never to go back. In a few weeks I had witnessed brutality and evil on a terrifying scale. . . . However, Rwanda did not go away, nor did the memory of Valentina and other survivors of genocide. I found myself endlessly questioning: how could this have happened? How could people butcher children? What kind of man can kill a child?

What did Keane feel then? Was it horror? Anguish? Shame? No doubt all of this and more. Later in the film, when we hear apologies and expression of shame from former US national security advisor Anthony Lake, the UN's Kofi Annan, and former US secretary of state Madeleine Albright, we are shown too their visits to the church at Nyarubuye, with its skeletons, moving testimony to a horrific past.

10 In *Pride, Shame, and Guilt* (Oxford: Oxford University Press, 1985),

Gabriele Taylor describes these three emotions as emotions of "self-assessment." She writes: "In experiencing any one of these emotions the person concerned believes of herself that she has deviated from some norm and that in doing so she has altered her standing in the world" (p. 1).

11 Shame does not require that others actually see us; it can arise as a feeling about how others might see us. It occurs at a moment of "social consciousness" in this broad sense. See Philip Fisher, *The Vehement Passions* (Princeton, NJ: Princeton University Press, 2002), pp. 65–68: "The feeling of shame occurs in the moment of becoming aware of others, the moment of a return to social consciousness . . ." (p. 67). Fisher emphasizes that shame, like an apology or embarrassment, comes after other feelings.

12 The relationship between shame and guilt is widely discussed in psychological and philosophical literature on shame. A recent, if brief, discussion can be found in Martha C. Nussbaum, *Hiding from Humanity: Disgust, Shame, and the Law* (Princeton, NJ: Princeton University Press, 2004), pp. 207–9, where she says:

> Guilt is a type of self-punishing anger, reacting to the perception that one has done a wrong or a harm. Thus, whereas shame focuses on defect or imperfection, and thus on some aspect of the very being of the person who feels it, guilt focuses on an action (or a wish to act), but need not extend to the entirety of the agent, seeing the agent as utterly inadequate.
>
> (p. 207)

This view does not mean that actions cannot give rise to feelings of shame. Nussbaum points out that there is a good deal of psychological literature about how guilt and shame "trigger" one another; see pp. 376–77, n. 99.

13 Shame is originally about nakedness and exposure, about appearing to others as we do, when it is inappropriate or wrong to do so. For us, however, there are many ways in which shame can arise. We can be ashamed of ourselves for looking the way we do, for saying what we have said at the wrong place or time, for having done what we should not have done, and on and on. Moreover, we can be ashamed of ourselves personally, our group, our country, or all of humankind. To feel

ashamed is to feel negatively about ourselves and others because we recognize that we have failed or are diminished by how we are or by what we have done. We seek to relieve that sense of being diminished by changing our character or by doing what we should. See Robert C. Roberts, *Emotions: An Essay in Aid of Moral Psychology* (Cambridge: Cambridge University Press, 2003), pp. 227–34: "Shame's consequent concern is to restore one's respectability or reduce one's disgrace" through self-justification, rationalization, or efforts to avoid similar situations in the future (p. 229).

14 The taking up of this external point of view is the result of a kind of moral imagination, of projection and construction. For discussion of the role of imagination or what he calls "phantasy" in complex emotions such as shame, see Richard Wollheim, *On the Emotions* (New Haven, CT: Yale University Press, 1999), pp. 148–224.

15 For an important account of shame, in all its richness and complexity, see Bernard Williams, *Shame and Necessity* (Berkeley, CA: University of California Press, 1993), pp. 77–102 and 219–23. One of Williams' aims is to show how the Kantian view of human psychology, action, and morality inadequately appreciates shame, the distinction between shame and guilt, and the notion of the moral self. As Williams points out, shame is connected with nakedness and exposure or with "being seen, inappropriately, by the wrong people, in the wrong condition. . . . The reaction is to cover oneself or to hide . . . . From this there is a spread of applications through various kinds of shyness or embarrass-ment" (p. 78). But shame is not just the being seen as naked, it is the feeling that we have about being seen; it is a "reaction of the subject to the consciousness of [a loss of power]" or, in Williams' citation of Gabriele Taylor, it is "the emotion of self-protection" (p. 220). See Taylor, *Pride, Shame, and Guilt*.

16 Nussbaum, *Hiding from Humanity*, especially chapter 4, provides a wide-ranging discussion, philosophical but based on psychological evidence, about related themes. She writes, for example, that shame "is a painful emotion responding to a sense of failure to attain some ideal state. . . . In shame, one feels inadequate, lacking some desired type of complete-ness or perfection" (p. 184).

17 Primo Levi, *The Drowned and the Saved*, trans. Raymond Rosenthal (New York: Summit Books, 1988), chapter 3, "Shame," pp. 70–87. Levi is cited

by several authors who have written about the Rwandan genocide. See, for example, Gourevitch, *We wish to inform you*, p. 275.

18 Levi, *The Drowned and the Saved*, pp. 72–73. For the quotation, see Primo Levi, *The Reawakening*, trans. Stuart Woolf (New York: Collier-Macmillan, 1965), p. 2.

19 For discussion of the standard of judgment or the import that the property or feature has about which we are ashamed, see Charles Taylor, "Self-interpreting Animals," *Human Agency and Language: Philosophical Papers I* (Cambridge: Cambridge University Press, 1985), pp. 53–55. See also Charles Taylor, "The Concept of a Person," *Human Agency and Language* (Cambridge: Cambridge University Press, 1985), pp. 109–12.

20 Also, of course, for how one looks, for features or characteristics one has, in general, that is, for perceived imperfections, deficiencies, or inadequacies. Since I am particularly interested in the shame I felt—and others feel—about our world and the omissions of the United States, other governments, and the United Nations with regard to intervening in genocides and failing to deal with the conditions that give rise to genocide, I focus here on shame that arises from actions or failures to act.

21 Levi, *The Drowned and the Saved*, pp. 76–78.

22 Ibid., pp. 77–78.

23 In such cases of failure, as Bernard Williams points out, we can feel both guilt and shame: "In a moment of cowardice, we let someone down; we feel guilty because we have let them down, ashamed because we have contemptibly fallen short of what we might have hoped of ourselves" (*Shame and Necessity*, p. 92). Williams notes that John Rawls discusses such a case in *A Theory of Justice* (Cambridge, MA: Harvard University Press, 1971), p. 445.

24 Primo Levi, *Survival in Auschwitz*, trans. Stuart Woolf (New York: Collier Books, 1961), pp. 128–29. The passage is quoted and discussed by Robert S. G. Gordon, *Primo Levi's Ordinary Virtues: From Testimony to Ethics* (Oxford: Oxford University Press, 2001), pp. 51–52. Gordon is primarily concerned with the role that looking and the look play for Levi.

25 Commenting on Levi's discussion of shame in *The Drowned and the Saved*, Richard Wollheim remarks that what Levi and the other prisoners were ashamed about, their wretched condition, was not something they did to themselves, whether we are talking about their attitude of self-interest or their horrible physical condition. Still, the shame was felt

and was somehow appropriate. "For we know," says Wollheim, "that lack of responsibility, or, for that matter, lack of intention, are fully compatible with deep, burning shame about what we have become" (*On the Emotions*, p. 199).

26 Charles Taylor discusses the fact that shame can be justified or not and that it can be more or less rational. See "Self-interpreting Animals," pp. 49–50.

27 One feels this shame about the world, I believe (at least I feel it), when reading books such as Imre Kertész's *Fateless*, Christopher Browning's *Ordinary Men*, and Jan Gross' *Neighbors* as well as Levi's *Survival in Auschwitz*. Wollheim discusses Levi's indication that there is such a shame "on behalf of humanity, of the whole human species" (*On the Emotions*, p. 200). He describes this deep feeling of shame as arising from a situation that brings into question one's very sense of self as an

> ongoing creature, related to his past, to his present, and to his future, in the ways in which we persons necessarily are. . . . Levi is further telling us, and out of his own experience, that life in the Lager, life as it was made, not, of course, by the prisoners, but for the prisoners by their captors, was of such an abject nature that merely to survive it and to go on existing, thinking of oneself as a person as life requires, was a permanent occasion for shame.
>
> (pp. 200–1)

So it was that "for many innocent men and women, the very broadest way they had of looking at themselves, that is, as persons, became so shot through with mistrust that they mistrusted everything that involved it" (p. 201).

28 The strategy to avoid using the term *genocide* to avoid the implications of such an admission, in view of the 1948 Genocide Convention, has been widely discussed. A clear and telling account can be found in Power, "*A Problem from Hell*", especially pp. 358–64. In *Ghosts of Rwanda* and excerpted in Power (pp. 363–64), there is a now famous State Department briefing, conducted by Christine Shelly on June 10, 1994, during which she is asked how she would describe the events taking place in Rwanda. Shelly answers that "we have every reason to believe that acts of genocide have occurred in Rwanda." She is then asked what the difference is between "acts of genocide" and "genocide," and after equivocating,

she is asked, "How many acts of genocide does it take to make a genocide?" Shelly answers: "Alan, that's just not a question that I'm in a position to answer."

29 Jay Cantor discusses the interview with Bomba in "Death and the Image," pp. 159–62, emphasizing Lanzmann's manipulation of the dialogue, the artifice of it all.

30 Or at least he appears to continue; in fact the scene was staged. Bomba had retired as a barber.

31 Claude Lanzmann, *Shoah: An Oral History of the Holocaust* (New York: Pantheon, 1985), pp. 111–17. This book contains the text of the film. The interview with Bomba was done in a Tel Aviv barbershop. During a visit to Indiana University, Lanzmann answered questions from members of my class on the Holocaust. I recall his saying that the interview with Bomba had to be done several times, until Bomba broke down and wept.

32 Levi, *The Drowned and the Saved*, pp. 81–85.

33 As Bernard Williams points out,

> Gabriele Taylor has well said that "shame is the emotion of self-protection," and in the experience of shame, one's whole being seems diminished or lessened . . . the expression of shame . . . is not just the desire to hide, or to hide my face, but the desire to disappear, not to be there.
>
> (*Shame and Necessity*, p. 89)

Shame, that is, seeks our non-existence, our total negation. And then, as Roberts says, it seeks to restore one's respectability or one's worthiness, either honestly or dishonestly; see above, note 13.

34 Rothman, *Documentary Film Classics*, pp. 58–59.

35 Ibid., pp. 61–62. Rothman associates these challenges with the fate of art and of our artfulness, so to speak:

> If we fail to look around us—fail to punish the guilty, fail to free the survivors, fail to lay the dead to rest, fail to recognize the executioners and victims that are everywhere in our world, fail to recognize the executioners and victims that, we, ourselves, are—that does not mean we are unaware of the horror, that our unawareness is the horror. It means that we are masters of the art of pretending not

to know what we cannot help knowing. If we remain deaf to the "endless cry," it means we are pretending not to hear.

(p. 63; see also pp. 65, 67–68)

36 As an emotion or feeling, shame is a way we are oriented to what we have done, to our features and character and the way we look, in terms of how others do or might see us. But it is also or can be a motivation to act. Feeling shame leads us to explain ourselves, to avoid being seen in a certain way, to apologize and ask for forgiveness. There is a moment in the film *Now, Voyager* when Jill, Charlotte Vale's niece, recalling how mean she had been to Charlotte (Betty Davis), hugs her and asks her for forgiveness—motivated by the shame she feels for having acted that way in the past. Or is guilt the motivation? Or both?

37 Levi, *The Drowned and the Saved*, pp. 86–87.

38 See Jean Améry, *At the Mind's Limits: Contemplations by a Survivor on Auschwitz and Its Realities*, trans. Sidney Rosenfeld and Stella P. Rosenfeld (Bloomington: Indiana University Press, 1980).

39 See Irving Greenberg, "Cloud of Smoke, Pillar of Fire: Judaism, Christianity, and Modernity after the Holocaust," in Eva Fleischner, ed., *Auschwitz: Beginning of a New Era?* (New York: Ktav Publishing, 1977), pp. 7–55; and Emil L. Fackenheim, "On the Life, Death, and Transfiguration of Martyrdom: The Jewish Testimony to the Divine Image in Our Time," *The Jewish Return into History* (New York: Schocken, 1978), pp. 234–51.

40 On Darfur, see, among numerous examples, Allen D. Hertzke, "The Shame of Darfur," *First Things* 156 (October 2005), 16–22, and especially Nicholas D. Kristof, "Genocide in Slow Motion," *The New York Review of Books* LIII:2 (February 9, 2006), 14–17. Kristof's review essay of two books on the genocide in Darfur begins with a litany:

During the Holocaust, the world looked the other way. . . . Only afterward did many people mourn the death of Anne Frank, construct Holocaust museums, and vow: Never Again. . . . The same paralysis occurred as Rwandans were being slaughtered in 1994. . . . Much the same has been true of the Western response to the Armenian genocide of 1915, the Cambodian genocide of the 1970s, and the Bosnian massacres of the 1990s. . . . And now the same tragedy is unfolding in Darfur, but this time we don't even have any sort of excuse.

(14)

41 As Bernard Williams suggests, shame can motivate positive responses as well as negative ones. The one who is ashamed of himself can "wish to hide or disappear" or "more positively, shame may be expressed in attempts to reconstruct or improve oneself" (*Shame and Necessity*, p. 90). Since shame arises from an act of omission or from some failing or defect (perceived by the agent as a defect, of course), and since it "elicits from others contempt or derision or avoidance," Williams adds, one's responses to shame seek reconciliation with others and with oneself, a sense of wholeness, communal and personal.

42 During the Rwandan genocide, Philippe Gaillard headed the delegation of the International Committee of the Red Cross in that country. He is one of the heroes of Linda Melvern's account in *A People Betrayed*, and he is interviewed extensively in *Ghosts of Rwanda*. At the end of the PBS film, Gaillard comments that he and his wife had not had children (nor seemed to want to have them), but upon their return, after the atrocities, they both felt the strong desire to have children and to produce life. The film ends with Gaillard's remark that he has never explained to his son that the boy's life is a response to genocide.

TWO   LOCATING MORAL SHAME

1 I will ignore the developmental aspects of shame and guilt, the claim that shame is characteristic of the young and immature and that guilt is a more mature emotion. I will also ignore here the distinction, made by Ruth Benedict in *The Chrysanthemum and the Sword: Patterns of Japanese Culture* (Boston: Houghton and Mifflin, 1946), between shame cultures and guilt cultures. Benedict is sometimes thought to have claimed that cultures are exclusively one or the other. In fact, although she claimed that in Japan shame is more dominant and in America guilt is more dominant, she did not argue that either culture was exclusively one or the other.

2 This distinction, between acknowledged and unacknowledged or "bypassed" shame was introduced by the psychologist Helen B. Lewis, *Shame and Guilt in Neurosis*. It has been widely adopted by psychologists, especially those who explore shame psychoanalytically, e.g., Donald Nathanson, A. P. Morrison, and Michael Lewis.

3 The argument for this claim is central to R. E. Lamb, "Guilt, Shame and Morality," *Philosophy and Phenomenological Research* XLIII:3 (March 1983),

329–46. Lamb introduces as data various features of guilt and shame that are revealed by linguistic usage and then formulates the distinction between the two in terms of the association of guilt with action, intention, and responsibility. Shame can be elicited by a larger variety of conditions but is produced by ridicule, laughter, or mockery in ways that guilt is not. Lamb argues against Herbert Morris that shame and guilt do not characterize two distinct moralities but rather "two systems of regulating behavior" (345). This does not mean that a particular "instance" of shame cannot support moral judgment and cannot be associated, in a particular case, with moral notions. What I propose about acknowledging shame as part of an effort at moral development, then, is compatible with Lamb's larger claims, since I am restricting what I say about shame to a very particular type of case. Still, Lamb's larger conclusion is too hasty. I believe that while it may be true that guilt, unlike shame, is *essentially* tied to responsibility, Lamb does not explore the diverse ways in which responsibility can be expressed, nor does he justify such a narrow view of morality that ties it so tightly to autonomy and rationality. The notion of morality which he uses seems very narrow indeed.

4 For example, Bernard Williams, in *Shame and Necessity*, argues that shame is morally relevant insofar as the standards applied by others arise from people whom the self respects (84, 100), i.e., carry some moral weight, and are part of one's social and moral world.

5 This is certainly the case with that kind of shame that Kathleen Woodward calls "traumatic shame," and which she associates with the shame of racism and the shame of gender, a shame that bewilders, confuses, and paralyzes. See Kathleen Woodward, "Traumatic Shame," 225–26.

6 See John Kekes, "Shame and Moral Progress," *Midwest Studies in Philosophy* XIII (1988) 282–96, and for critical comment Robert Metcalf, "Balancing the Senses of Shame and Humor," *Journal of Social Philosophy* 35:3 (fall 2004), 432–47.

7 Jennifer C. Manion, "Girls Blush, Sometimes: Gender, Moral Agency, and the Problem of Shame."

8 T. M. Scanlon, in a discussion of moral criticism and guilt, suggests that "shame is just a matter of feeling inferior or deficient in some respect" and claims that "self-reproach is always grounds for shame. One can feel ashamed of one's height or clumsiness as well as one's

misbehavior or one's spelling errors, mistakes in mathematics, or unwary moves in chess. But not all of these things are possible grounds of guilt" (*What We Owe to Each Other*, Cambridge, MA: Belknap Press of Harvard University Press, 1998, pp. 269–70). But Scanlon then distinguishes shame and embarrassment from guilt, insofar as "guilt requires negative self-evaluation of a particular kind," i.e., "the attitude of taking one's rational self-governance to have been faulty" (270). This is "self-reproach" in a technical sense, where one is responsible for the fault, unlike one's height or weight or clumsiness. One can agree with Scanlon here; what he says, however, does not rule out that there are cases of shame which are a matter of rational failure. In fact, in saying that self-reproach is always a grounds for shame, he is admitting that when it is, the shame is about a failure of ours, although the failure may be harder to locate than in the case of guilt.

9 There are many accounts of what it is like to experience shame. For a survey of features, see Johann A. Klaassen, "The Taint of Shame: Failure, Self-Distress, and Moral Growth," *Journal of Social Philosophy* 32:3 (summer 2001), 182–86. See also, S. Miller, *The Shame Experience*.

10 For a succinct description of what the experience of shame is like, see John Sabini and Maury Silver, "In Defense of Shame," 3; this account draws on June Price Tangney, "Moral Affect: The Good, the Bad, and the Ugly," *Journal of Personality and Social Psychology* 61 (1991), 598–607, p. 599.

11 Kathleen Woodward claims that "the private experience of reading [Toni] Morrison's *The Bluest Eye* underwrites a sense of shame that is intensely moral, a shame associated with civic responsibility and thus with dignity . . ." ("Traumatic Shame," 230). Woodward brings to the arena of racial shame a kind of argumentation, for shame as transformative and morally relevant, that others have claimed in the arena of feminist thinking.

12 On humiliation, see William Ian Miller, *Humiliation and Other Essays on Honor, Social Discomfort, and Violence* (Ithaca, NY: Cornell University Press, 1993), chapters 4 and 5.

13 Recall the passage from Primo Levi, *The Drowned and the Saved*, cited in chapter 1.

14 There are philosophers who argue, in a way similar to this, for the moral relevance of shame to the situation of women and minorities,

even though the faults for which they are made to feel ashamed are fabricated and grounded in bias or oppression. See, for example, Jennifer C. Manion, "Girls Blush, Sometimes. . . ." et al.

15 This might be said too of course about the extent and degree of poverty, hunger, and destitution in the world and of the disregard for the environment.

16 One might ask the same question about other emotions like fear or anger as well, but guilt is especially appropriate, since it is so closely tied to shame and the family of self-critical emotions associated with both.

17 Lewis' original work is presented in *Shame and Guilt in Neurosis*. Others who have appropriated this way of marking the distinction include Michael Lewis, *Shame*, and June Tangney and Ronda Dearing, *Shame and Guilt*. But there are many others, both psychologists and philosophers.

18 An exception is Ilham Dilman, "Shame, Guilt and Remorse," *Philosophical Investigations* 22:4 (October 1999), 312–29, much of which involves a clarification and elaboration of Bernard Williams' discussion in chapter 4 of *Shame and Necessity*.

19 See above, note 4.

20 In chapter 1, pages 21–22, I noted that Primo Levi calls this a "shame of the world."

21 There are of course features or characteristics for which we are made to feel ashamed which we cannot change or cannot normally change. Here I am thinking of our racial background or our religious background. We can try to "hide" from these aspects of our identity, but even this may in fact be very difficult, if not impossible, to do. Moreover, in such cases, the point of the shame is not to find ways to avoid our identities in the face of prejudice and persecution but rather to alter how we respond to the treatment of others and hence how we accept our identities and deal with the hatred or resentment of others.

22 Tangney and Dearing, *Shame and Guilt*, 126 and chapter 8.

23 Tangney and Dearing, *Shame and Guilt*, 126.

24 I thank Jonathan Rosenbaum and James Naremore for introducing me to this essay and providing me with a copy of it.

25 James Agee, "America, Look at Your Shame!" *Oxford American* (Jan./Feb. 2003).

26 Michael Lewis, *Shame*, pp. 149–53.

27 See Terry George, *Hotel Rwanda: Bringing the True Story of an African Hero to Film* (New York: Newmarket Press, 2005), pp. 192–93.

28 Primo Levi, "Shemá," in Hilda Schiff (ed.), *Holocaust Poetry* (New York: St. Martin's Press, 1995), p. 205; reprinted from Primo Levi, *Collected Poems*, trans. Ruth Feldman and Brian Swan (London: Faber, 1988). In a paper for a course on Levinas, Darla Martin-Gorski reminded me of this poem of Primo Levi.

THREE FILM, LITERATURE, AND THE RAMIFICATION OF SHAME

1 Historically speaking, media coverage and especially photographs in newspapers and magazines and footage on television have played an important role in making people in the West aware of what is going on elsewhere and in generating a sense of urgency and concern about helping those in need. In the case of the Kurdish crisis in 1991–93, the Rwandan genocide in 1994, the crisis in Somalia, and those in Bosnia and Kosovo, media coverage played a major role in shaping public opinion—for example, in Great Britain and the United States—that influenced policy decisions. For discussion, see S. L. Carruthers, *The Media at War* (London: Macmillan, 1999); L. Minear, C. Scott, and T. G.Weiss, *The News Media, Civil War, and Humanitarian Action* (Boulder, Colorado: Lynne Reinner, 1996); M. Shaw, *Civil Society and Media in Global Crises* (London: Pinter, 1996).

2 There has been a tendency, among historians and others, to treat the Nazi Holocaust as a paradigm and hence to examine every subsequent atrocity and massacre in its light. Mark Mazower, in a recent essay, argues against such a strategy:

> the rise of Holocaust studies has seen the Final Solution—genocide at the hands of a highly organized state apparatus—turned into a paradigm for understanding modern violence, if not modern life altogether. . . . The cumulative effect of these developments has been to highlight the central role played by the violent state, and to see modern mass violence in terms derived from the experience of a small number of historiographically dominant European paradigms. It is, however, questionable how far these paradigms allow us to

understand the origins of such diverse events as the massacres that accompanied the partition of India in 1947, la Violencia in Cold War Colombia, or the expulsion of ethnic Germans from Eastern Europe after 1945. . . . Perhaps the time has come . . . to reconsider the usefulness of the Holocaust as a historical benchmark for modern mass violence, and to ask how useful the categories most recently associated with it—namely, genocide and ethnic cleansing—are as instruments of historical analysis.

("Violence and the State in the Twentieth Century," *American Historical Review* 107:4 [October 2002], 1159–160)

3 In "Traumatic Shame" Kathleen Woodward uses Jean-Paul Sartre's famous account of shame in *Being and Nothingness*, Virginia Woolf's *A Room of One's Own*, and Toni Morrison's *The Bluest Eye* to explore what she calls the "cultural politics of shame" (211). These literary works represent different perspectives on shame and on the role of shame in a "cultural politics," i.e., as symptomatic of moral agency and social roles, among other things. She also discusses how television exploits shame for political-cultural purposes. In this chapter, I do not deny that there are political roles that Holocaust representations and the representations of genocide and atrocity play, and that the dialectic of these artifacts with shame, internally and with their audiences, have a political-cultural role to play. But I focus on the way in which the portrayals themselves ramify and complicate the audience's shame and our shame, with regard to the moral character of our situation in a genocidal world.

4 Stanley Cavell, "Fred Astaire Asserts the Right to Praise," *Philosophy the Day After Tomorrow* (Cambridge, MA: Harvard University Press, 2005), pp. 61–82, especially 76. The Astaire routine that Cavell examines is from *The Bandwagon* (1953), directed by Vincent Minnelli. The full account occurs on pp. 72–79.

5 When reading a book on the history of slavery in America, such as David Brion Davis' stunning *Inhuman Bondage: The Rise and Fall of Slavery in the New World* (New York: Oxford University Press, 2006), the sense of moral failure is palpable, the shame not easy to avoid. In Cavell's case, the rebuke is more subtle and nuanced, the shame easy to miss.

6 Does the distortion or fabrication have to have a certain result in order for us to be ashamed at being seduced by it? The issue is complicated.

See Stefan Maechler's comprehensive and detailed exposé, *The Wilkomirski Affair* (New York: Schocken, 2001).

7 One natural response to being put to shame is to blame the messenger rather than to accept honestly the message. This is one way of reading the Athenian response to Socrates' commitment to questioning his fellow Athenians for their own good; Plato alludes to the trial and execution of Socrates in book VII of the *Republic*, when he says that the prisoners in the Cave, when informed about their confusion about what is right and just, may very well malign the released prisoner who informs them and even put him on trial.

8 In later notes on the film, Breen required that the drunkenness in the bar scene be toned down, that Gloria Graham's character not be portrayed as a prostitute and the man who interrupts her and Mitchell in her apartment not be portrayed as her client, and that Samuels, the Jew, not be portrayed as gay. He also required that the final scene, which originally had Monty gunned down by military police, be rewritten.

9 Some might call this emotion "guilt," especially insofar as it is elicited by a recollection of the death of his son. But, I would suggest, this is one of those cases where it is hard to distinguish between guilt and shame. Moreover, I take Nazerman to be responding to a sense of his whole life as worthless and without meaning.

10 *The Pawnbroker* is based on the 1961 novel of the same name by Edward Lewis Wallant. Like the novel, the film has obvious Christological overtones. It suggests that only an ultimate sacrifice can redeem us from extraordinary pain and suffering. The act must incorporate both a dimension of selflessness, expressed in the film by Jesus' being shot in order to save Nazerman, and one that penetrates below the layers of anger and rage in order to expose the fundamental pain for what it is, expressed in the film by Nazerman's impaling his hand on the spindle in the pawn shop after Jesus' death. The latter scene is perhaps the most memorable in the film, with Rod Steiger's silent shriek and agonized facial expression as he forces his hand down onto the spindle—off camera—and it penetrates through his palm. Jesus and Nazerman—is he a Nazerite or the man from Nazereth? Or both?—are two sides of the redeeming victim.

11 Another film, one that I think is a beautiful achievement, that more

subtly explores the influence of repressed shame in the lives of Holocaust survivors and does so with remarkable sensitivity and complexity, is *Enemies: A Love Story*, based on a novel by Isaac Bashevis Singer and directed by Paul Mazursky. Everything about this film is extraordinary: the screenplay, the acting, the direction, the music and sets, and the tone. Unlike *The Pawnbroker*, *Enemies* does not lapse into melodrama or allow itself excesses. It is humorous, dark, and nuanced.

12 *Two Women* (1999; director, Tahmineh Milani; Iran); *The Circle* (2000; director, Jafar Panahi; Iran); *Fire* (1996; director, Deepa Mehta; India); *Osama* (2003; director, Siddiq Barmak; Afghanistan).

13 See Miriam Bratu Hansen, "*Schindler's List* Is Not *Shoah*: Second Commandment, Popular Modernism, and Public Memory," in Yosefa Loshitzky (ed.), *Spielberg's Holocaust: Critical Perspectives on* Schindler's List (Bloomington, IN: Indiana University Press, 1997), pp. 77–103.

14 A good example of an attempt to come to grips with classic Hollywood film as both bound by its own conventions and yet as a creative attempt to articulate deep human and ethical themes is Stanley Cavell's readings of the two genres, as he calls them, those of the "comedies of remarriage" and of the "melodramas of the unknown woman." See Stanley Cavell, *Pursuits of Happiness* (Cambridge, MA: Harvard University Press, 1981) and *Contesting Tears* (Chicago: University of Chicago Press, 1996), as well as *Cities of Words* (Cambridge, MA: Harvard University Press, 2004).

15 Aryeh Lev Stollman, *The Far Euphrates* (New York: Riverhead Books, 1997), p. 4.

16 I am indebted to a paper presented by Emily Budick on Stollman's novel at the Conference on Holocaust Representation at the College of William and Mary, May 2006.

FOUR BEYOND SHAME: EMOTIONAL REACTION AND MORAL RESPONSE

1 In the film *Caché* (Hidden) (Michael Haneke, 2005) the Moroccan man, Majid, who had known the main character, Georges, in childhood and was the object of Georges' jealousy, commits suicide by slitting his throat in front of Georges, whom he called to his home to witness the act. Majid's suicide is an expression of his profound sense of shame and loss of face, when he is charged with harassing Georges and his wife

and discovers that it has been his son (we presume this) who has been doing it, i.e., after Majid's denials, he discovers that there has been harassment and that his son has been responsible. The depth of his loss of face and of his sense of shame is so great that nothing remains but for him to take his life, and to do so before his prosecutor, whom he believes has done him a great wrong but before whom his sense of dignity has been compromised. The scene is shocking, and leaves us stunned. Even before one whom one hates or towards whom one is indifferent, one can feel such a traumatic sense of failure that it could lead one, as a matter of honor and integrity, to take one's life—no longer to go on living but to remove oneself from the eyes of others permanently.

2 Thomas J. Scheff, "Shame and the Social Bond: A Sociological Perspective," *Sociological Theory* 18:1 (March 2000), 84–99.

3 For another example of shame as a collective, national response, consider Winston Churchill's famous remark of September 1938, in response to the policy of appeasing Hitler, from a statement before Czech journalists, that "France and Britain had to choose between war and shame. They chose shame, but they will get war, too." Cited by Leslie Hill, *Blanchot: Extreme Contemporary* (London: Routledge, 1997), p. 45; also, Hugh Dalton, *The Fateful Years* (London: Frederick Muller, 1957), p. 198.

4 One such film is Bertrand Tavernier's remarkable and beautiful 1989 film *Life and Nothing But*. It is one year after the end of World War I, and the main character, Major Dellaplane, has the responsibility of identifying thousands of French soldiers, some in hospitals and holding centers, others found dead on the battlefield of Verdun. He is a cynical servant of those who have suffered and died and of their relatives who seek helplessly to honor their memory. As he carries on his grim task with precision and rigor, a thorn in the side of the French military and government, the latter seek to placate themselves and the nation by using one anonymous dead soldier to represent the 1,500,000 who died, as the "unknown soldier." Dellaplane faces the reality of death and suffering; his very commitment to identifying the victims rather than to allow them to remain unknown is a chastisement to his superiors who seek to use one "unknown" fallen soldier as a vehicle for forgetting, for a national amnesia.

5 This is also the theme of Vasily Grossman's *Life and Fate*, his epic realist novel about the battle of Stalingrad, which shows the suffering of common people at the hands of two competing totalitarianisms—Hitler and Stalin. The book is a scathing indictment of war and the ideologies that drive us to war.

6 This risk becomes evident when one reads Simon Critchley's praise for the film in Critchley's discussion of it in his book on Wallace Stevens and the everyday, *Things Merely Are* (London: Routledge, 2005). The bypassing of grand narratives and themes in favor of allowing the prosaic and mundane to present themselves in all their distinctiveness is also a theme of Michael André Bernstein, *Foregone Conclusions* (Berkeley, CA: University of California Press, 1994); it is a theme that Bernstein finds in the writings of Robert Musil. It is also a feature of Siegfried Kracauer's *Theory of Film* (Princeton, NJ: Princeton University Press, 1997). See my discussion in *Interim Judaism*.

7 Virtually every psychological study of shame and guilt remarks that shame regularly leads to negative outcomes—narcissistic behavior, blame of others, depression, anger and rage, and even suicide. There is some debate about whether guilt or shame is a more adaptive or productive emotion. Both are thought to have a self-protective function, but often enough, as for Tangney and Dearing, for example, guilt is claimed to be more beneficial. At least one reason is shame's global nature, that it targets the self as a whole and hence is not specific enough to elicit precise, corrective behavior.

8 There is a gripping example of shame turning into murderous rage in Claude Chabrol's film *Le Cérémonie*. A young maid and housekeeper, deeply ashamed of her illiteracy, which she struggles to keep hidden but which is eventually discovered by the family for which she works, is incited by her resentment toward that bourgeois family and provoked by an embittered postal clerk who befriends her. In a fit of rage and frightening glee, the two women murder the members of the family, shooting them all with shotguns.

9 One thing that shame can lead to is confession. Günter Grass, in an interview given to the *Frankfurter Allgemeine Zeitung*, said he volunteered for submarine service toward the end of World War II but was called up instead to serve in the Waffen-SS in the eastern city of Dresden. He said: "It weighed on me. My silence over all these years is one of the reasons I

wrote this book [his memoirs of his experiences during the war]." At the time, he was not concerned by his membership in a branch of the SS, but after the war, he said, he was overwhelmed by the burden of the shame. If Grass is to be believed, the publication of the memoir was motivated by the need to break the silence and make public the truth about his past.

10 Larry May, in *Shared Responsibility*, argues that when ashamed of being a member of a group, one should resign membership or change the group's behavior. Surely, doing one or the other might be morally responsible and beneficial.

11 The role of moral psychology and emotional development in the process of moral education has been widely discussed. It is often associated with figures such as Aristotle and Hume. Among a number of important works, see essays reprinted in John McDowell, *Mind, Value, and Reality* (Cambridge, MA: Harvard University Press, 1998) and Sabina Lovibond, *Ethical Formation* (Cambridge, MA: Harvard University Press, 2002). Also, Annette Baier, *Postures of the Mind* (Minneapolis: University of Minnesota Press, 1985) and *Moral Prejudices* (Cambridge, MA: Harvard University Press, 1994).

12 See Peter Singer's classic essay, "Famine, Affluence, and Morality," *Philosophy and Public Affairs* 1 (1972), 229–44 (frequently reprinted). Also Peter Singer, *Practical Ethics* (Cambridge: Cambridge University Press, 1979) and *One World: The Ethics of Globalization* (New Haven, CT: Yale University Press, 2002).

13 See also Robert E. Goodin, *Protecting the Vulnerable: A Reanalysis of Our Social Responsibilities* (Chicago: University of Chicago Press, 1985).

14 Nicholas J. Wheeler notes how Michael Ignatieff links a sense of humanitarian responsibility to all with the Holocaust and the shame of having abandoned the Jews:

> Western states should have rescued Rwandans in 1994 for reasons of humanity. This is the importance of Michael Ignatieff's observation that what connects the "zone of safety" in the West to the "zone of danger" in places like Africa is "a narrative of compassion . . . that the problems of other people, no matter how far away, are of concern to all of us." He argues that this moral universalism was forged out of the horrors of the Holocaust and that it is predicated on humanity's

shame at its "abandonment of the Jews," which created "a new kind of crime: the crime against humanity."

> (*Saving Strangers*, 302; citing Michael Ignatieff,
> *The Warrior's Honor: Ethnic War and the Modern Conscience*
> [London: Chatto & Windus, 1998], pp. 4–5, 19)

15 An excellent example of a powerful argument in behalf of global justice is Thomas Pogge's *World Poverty and Human Rights* (Cambridge: Polity Press, 2002).

Bibliography

Agee, James. "America, Look at Your Shame!" *Oxford American* (Jan./Feb. 2003).

Aldrich, Virgil C. "An Ethics of Shame." *Ethics* 50 (1939), 57–77.

Améry, Jean. *At the Mind's Limits: Contemplations by a Survivor on Auschwitz and Its Realities*, trans. Sidney Rosenfeld and Stella P. Rosenfeld. Bloomington: Indiana University Press, 1980.

Avisar, Ilan. *Screening the Holocaust: Cinema's Images of the Unimaginable*. Bloomington: Indiana University Press, 1988.

Barnett, Michael. *Eyewitness to a Genocide: The United Nations and Rwanda*. Ithaca, NY: Cornell University Press, 2002.

Boonin, Leonard. "Guilt, Shame and Morality." *Journal of Value Inquiry* 17 (1983), 295–304.

Broucek, Francis. *Shame and the Self*. New York: Guilford Press, 1991.

Calhoun, Cheshire. "An Apology for Moral Shame." *The Journal of Political Philosophy* 12:2 (2004), 127–46.

Cantor, Jay. "Death and the Image." In *On Giving Birth to One's Own Mother: Essays on Art and Society*. New York: Alfred A. Knopf, 1991. Pp. 143–77.

Colombat, André Pierre. *The Holocaust in French Film*. Metuchen, NJ: Scarecrow Press, 1993.

Dallaire, Roméo. *Shake Hands with the Devil: The Failure of Humanity in Rwanda*. Toronto: Random House, 2003.

Darwin, Charles. *The Expression of the Emotions in Man and Animals*. Stilwell, KS: Digireads, 2005 (originally 1872).

Deigh, John. "Shame and Self-Esteem: A Critique." *Ethics* 93 (January 1983), 225–45.

Destexhe, Alain. *Rwanda and Genocide in the Twentieth Century*. New York: New York University Press, 1995.

Dilman, Ilham. "Shame, Guilt and Remorse." *Philosophical Investigations* 22:4 (October 1999), 312–29.

Elias, Norbert. *The Civilizing Process*. Vols.1–3. New York: Pantheon, 1978, 1982, 1983.

Fackenheim, Emil L. "On the Life, Death, and Transfiguration of Martyrdom: The Jewish Testimony to the Divine Image in Our Time." In *The Jewish Return into History*. New York: Schocken, 1978. Pp. 234–51.

—— *To Mend the World*. New York: Schocken, 1982.

Fisher, Philip. *The Vehement Passions*. Princeton, NJ: Princeton University Press, 2002.

Goffman, Erving. *Interaction Ritual*. New York: Anchor, 1967.

—— *Stigma*. Englewood Cliffs, NJ: Prentice-Hall, 1963.

—— *Presentation of Self in Everyday Life*. New York: Anchor, 1959.

Goodin, Robert E. *Protecting the Vulnerable: A Reanalysis of Our Social Responsibilities*. Chicago: University of Chicago Press, 1985.

Gordon, Robert S. G. *Primo Levi's Ordinary Virtues: From Testimony to Ethics*. Oxford: Oxford University Press, 2001.

Gourevitch, Philip. *We wish to inform you that tomorrow we will be killed with our families*. New York: Farrar, Straus and Giroux, 1998.

Greenberg, Irving. "Cloud of Smoke, Pillar of Fire: Judaism, Christianity, and Modernity after the Holocaust." In Eva Fleischner, ed. *Auschwitz: Beginning of a New Era?* New York: Ktav Publishing, 1977. Pp. 7–55.

Grossman, Vasily. *Life and Fate*. New York: NYRB Classics, 2006. (1st ed. 1960).

Klaassen, Johann A. "The Taint of Shame: Failure, Self-Distress, and Moral Growth." *Journal of Social Philosophy* 32:3 (summer 2001), 174–96.

Lamb, R. E. "Guilt, Shame, and Morality." *Philosophy and Phenomenological Research* XLIII:3 (March 1983), 329–46.

Levi, Primo. *The Drowned and the Saved*, trans. Raymond Rosenthal. New York: Summit Books, 1988.

—— *The Reawakening*, trans. Stuart Woolf. New York: Collier-Macmillan, 1965.

Lewis, Helen B. *Shame and Guilt in Neurosis*. New York: International Universities Press, 1971.

—— (ed.) *The Role of Shame in Symptom Formation*. Hillsdale, NJ: Erlbaum, 1987.

Lewis, Michael. *Shame: The Exposed Self*. New York: The Free Press, 1992; 1995.

Lynd, Helen M. *On Shame and the Search for Identity*. New York: Harcourt Brace, 1958.

Manion, Jennifer C. "Girls Blush, Sometimes: Gender, Moral Agency, and the Problem of Shame." *Hypatia* 18:3 (fall 2003), 21–41.

—— "The Moral Relevance of Shame." *American Philosophical Quarterly* 39:1 (2002), 73–90.

Melvern, Linda. *Conspiracy to Murder: The Rwandan Genocide*. London: Verso, 2004.

—— *A People Betrayed: The Role of the West in Rwanda's Genocide*. London: Zed Books, 2000.

Metcalf, Robert. "Balancing the Senses of Shame and Humor." *Journal of Social Philosophy* 35:3 (fall 2004), 432–47.

—— "The Truth of Shame-Consciousness in Freud and Phenomenology." *Journal of Phenomenological Psychology* 31:1 (2000), 1–18.

Miller, S. *The Shame Experience*. Hillsdale, NJ: Erlbaum, 1985.

Miller, William Ian. *Humiliation and Other Essays on Honor, Social Discomfort, and Violence*. Ithaca, NY: Cornell University Press, 1993.

Morrison, A. P. *Shame: The Underside of Narcissism*. Hillsdale, NJ: Erlbaum, 1989.

Nathanson, Donald L. *Shame and Pride: Affect, Sex, and the Birth of the Self*. New York: W. W. Norton & Company, 1992.

—— (ed.) *The Many Faces of Shame*. New York: Guilford Press, 1987.

Nussbaum, Martha C. *Hiding from Humanity: Disgust, Shame, and the Law*. Princeton, NJ: Princeton University Press, 2004.

O'Hear, Anthony. "Guilt and Shame as Moral Concepts." *Proceedings of the Aristotelian Society* 77 (1976–1977), 73–86.

Piers, Gerhart and Milton B. Singer. *Shame and Guilt: A Psychoanalytic and a Cultural Study*. Springfield, IL: Charles C. Thomas Publisher, 1953.

Power, Samantha. *"A Problem from Hell": America and the Age of Genocide*. New York: HarperCollins, 2002.

Prunier, Gérard. *The Rwanda Crisis: History of a Genocide*. New York: Columbia University Press, 1997.

Roberts, Robert C. *Emotions: An Essay in Aid of Moral Psychology*. Cambridge: Cambridge University Press, 2003.

Rothman, William. *Documentary Film Classics*. Cambridge: Cambridge University Press, 1997.

Sabini, John and Maury Silver. "In Defense of Shame: Shame in the Context of Guilt and Embarrassment." *Journal of the Theory of Social Behaviour* 27:1 (1997), 1–15.

Scanlon, T. M. *What We Owe to Each Other*. Cambridge, MA: Belknap Press of Harvard University Press, 1998.

Scheff, Thomas J. "Shame in Self and Society." *Symbolic Interaction* 26:2 (2003), 239–62.

—— "Shame and the Social Bond: A Sociological Theory." *Sociological Theory* 18:1 (March 2000), 84–99.

Sedgwick, Eve Kosofsky and Adam Frank (eds.) *Shame and Its Sisters: A Silvan Tomkins Reader*. Durham, NC: Duke University Press, 1995.

Tangney, June Price and Ronda L. Dearing. *Shame and Guilt*. New York: The Guilford Press, 2002.

Tangney, June Price and Kurt W. Fischer (eds.) *Self-Conscious Emotions: The Psychology of Shame, Guilt, Embarrassment and Pride*. New York: Guilford Press, 1995.

Taylor, Charles. "Self-interpreting Animals." In *Human Agency and Language: Philosophical Papers I*. Cambridge: Cambridge University Press, 1985. Pp. 53–55.

—— "The Concept of a Person." In *Human Agency and Language*. Cambridge: Cambridge University Press, 1985. Pp. 109–12.

Taylor, Gabriele. *Pride, Shame, and Guilt*. New York: Oxford University Press, 1985.

Velleman, J. David. "The Genesis of Shame." *Philosophy and Public Affairs* 30: 1 (Winter, 2001), 27–52. Reprinted in Velleman, *Self to Self*. Cambridge: Cambridge University Press. Pp. 45–69.

Walsh, W. H. "Pride, Shame and Responsibility." *The Philosophical Quarterly* 20:78 (January 1970), 1–13.

Wheeler, Nicholas J. *Saving Strangers: Humanitarian Intervention in International Society*. Oxford: Oxford University Press, 2000.

Williams, Bernard. *Shame and Necessity*. Berkeley, CA: University of California Press, 1993.

Wollheim, Richard. *On the Emotions*. New Haven, CT: Yale University Press, 1999.

Woodward, Kathleen. "Traumatic Shame: Toni Morrison, Televisual Culture, and the Cultural Politics of the Emotions." *Cultural Critique* 46 (fall 2000), 210–40.

Index